Growing Up
With a
Soul Full of Nature

One man's story of a childhood filled
with nature as a teacher

Tim Corcoran
And Jean Sage

Will —
I hope to work
with you again.
Get out into the woods
its the best place to be!

Tim Corcoran

Contact the author in care of Dog Ear Publishing.

First published by Dog Ear Publishing
4010 W. 86th Street, Ste H
Indianapolis, IN 46268
www.dogearpublishing.net

ISBN: 978-145750-156-2

This book is printed on acid-free paper.

Printed in the United States of America

ACKNOWLEDGMENTS

I would like to thank Jean Sage, my wife, for helping me to put my life experiences into words, John Wall for initially inspiring me to write out my story, and Julie Boettler for her contribution in editing this book.

I am eternally grateful for all of the hard work, long hours and dedication put into making this book come to life.

DEDICATION

A being like "Bear" only comes along once in a lifetime. I feel blessed to have traveled his life's journey with him. I feel I have lived with a being of pure love. What a teacher and inspiration Bear has been for me.

Bear was my working partner in my school, "Headwaters Outdoor School". He opened hearts, and that allows nature to flow in, thus making the connection to nature natural, deepseated and forever. I will forever miss my dog, Bear, both friend and partner.

Much love to you on your journey, my friend.
Tim Corcoran

"One of the penalties of an ecological education is that one lives alone in a world of wounds. Much of the damage inflicted on land is quite invisible to laymen. An Ecologist must either harden his shell and make believe that the consequences of science are none of his business, or he must be the doctor who sees the marks of death in a community that believes itself well and does not want to be told otherwise. "

-Aldo Leopold, A Sand County Almanac

CONTENTS

"Never doubt that a small group of thoughtful, committed citizens can change the world; indeed, it's the only thing that ever does."

-Margaret Mead

INTRODUCTION

Finding refuge in nature saved my life.

One of the mysteries of life is that we don't really know why someone thrives and another doesn't. I know people who have risen above their addictions, despair and poverty and become happy, sober and financially secure. How did they or I do it? I can't speak to the "they", but I found my sanity at an early age by being able to literally feel the earth. Perhaps it was because I was so young, and still relatively unformed by societal dictates, that I could feel the energy of all things, and I knew then what has become common knowledge now, that "all things are connected".

The great religions and philosophies have for centuries talked about the energies within all things, and specifically human beings in terms of the seven chakras, the seven sacraments, the Kabbalah Tree of Life etc. The root, or tribal energy at the base of the spine, connects us with our tribe and with the earth. When we lose that initial, primal connection we lose our way. As our tribe or family or culture dictates its perception of reality, we incorporate those prejudices and beliefs until we are old enough to experience and form our own beliefs.

Breaking from the pack requires a solitary, internal journey. It's the crisis time that sent Jesus into the wilderness for forty days, and Moses to the mountain, and the Buddha to the Bodhi Tree, where he sat until he attained enlightenment. All the great teachers who changed the way we perceive the world went into nature. They returned to their roots both physically and psychically in order to move through and above the outdated laws of their tribe.

I have been fortunate to have never lost my connection with nature. Being in it and of it and teaching others how to appreciate it, rather than fear it, has been my life's work. I created Headwaters Outdoor School in Mount Shasta, California in 1992 to help people come back to the one source that heals us all.

The stories in this book are about my experiences growing up in nature, and being allowed to have adventures in the wild that were dangerous, but character-forming. My parents never said no to my need to be outdoors. I hope through the progression of these stories they will inspire not only young kids, but also inspire the parents, who may have forgotten the importance of allowing enough play time in the backyard or the woods for their children and themselves.

I would like to inspire adults to become kids again by building shelters and climbing trees, and sitting for an afternoon under a tree with no, absolutely no distractions. It's time for everyone to get dirty and muddy again. You will be amazed at what inspires you and what no longer resonates as true.

It is my hope to remind people through my life's observations that it is your birthright to be connected to nature. Reclaim your birthright and make the connection. If you are already connected to nature then deepen that relationship. The wonderful thing about the natural world is the deeper you go the more you learn, and the more you'll want to be of service, and the more fulfilled you'll feel. There is no end to how deep you can go in nature. Nature will just keep opening wider.

I tell my students, and it's worth saying here - you will know you have succeeded in life when on your death bed you can answer "yes" to the question: Is the world a better place because you were in it? If you can, and if you do, oh my what a life you lived.

"Until one is committed there is hesitancy, the chance to draw back, always ineffectiveness. Concerning all acts of initiative (and creation) there is one elementary truth, the ignorance of which kills countless ideas and splendid plans; that the moment one definitely commits oneself, then providence moves too. All sorts of things occur to help one that would never otherwise have occurred. A whole stream of events issues from the decision, raising in one's favor all manner of unforeseen incidents and meetings and material assistance, which no man could have dreamt would have come his way. Whatever you can do, or dream you can, begin it. Boldness has genius, magic and power in it."

-Goethe

COMING HOME TO NATURE

Chapter One

There were only two good things I learned from the Catholic religion. The first was learning about St. Francis of Assisi. He was my hero because he could talk to animals. He was the subject of my major project in catechism. I was grateful that my father was disenchanted with the church when I was a kid as well. He said that he was tired of the priests, and he was really tired of listening to them tell him how bad I was for cutting catechism to go to the woods - nothing like ignoring the wisdom of one of the religion's great saints.

The second good thing was that I learned about miracles. I take miracles seriously. Especially the everyday kind of miracles that are ever-present in nature. The kind of miracle we hear about these days, like a female gorilla taking care of a human baby that fell into its cage at a zoo, or the female lion in the wild who nursed lost gem buck babies. Those are the kind of miracles that teach us that all things are connected.

There is a lot of confusion between the meaning of religion and the essence of spirituality. I know people who have a genuine spiritual practice that don't go to church, and I know people who go to church and quote the bible, yet have no idea what spirituality is about.

I work with kids who come from dogmatic, religious families who have a hard time reconciling what they see and hear, with what they feel in terms of spirit and spirituality. I support them to practice what they believe in and tell them to find what's good in the teachings. Find the common thread which speaks to us all.

It's important to feel that there is a greater power at work in the universe, and that we are not just machines who grow up, go to work, have a family or not, and die. That's a pretty depressing way to look at life. I try to instill in them the source of the greater power, and the spirit that moves in all things is present in the trees and plants, animals and flowers, and every thing you can see, feel, touch and smell on this earth, and in all the things we can't see.

One of my teachers used to speak about the "doorways" into nature. These are the places where a person feels safe enough to open up to the mysteries of the physical and non-physical realms. Mountain-climbing, hiking, fishing, camping, painting, taking pictures, botanizing and bird-watching are just some examples of those doorways that lead to a deeper connection with the earth.

As more people move into urban areas, the shift in population density from just twenty years ago has created a nature deficiency, which in my mind is as much a crisis as childhood obesity and depression. Coming home to nature is about being aware of the rhythms of the earth. It's about paying attention to full moons, seeing the trees bud in the spring and lose their leaves in the fall.

I believe that part of the reason global warming has exceeded scientist's estimations is because people have no connection to the earth. Urban dwellers don't know what it's like when there is too little rain, until the lakes and reservoirs become critically low and they can't go boating, or they are *told* to limit watering their lawns.

When all the best waterfront areas are blighted by hundreds of people living in condos, the wildlife and the underground reserves of water are threatened – but the views are fabulous, and so we push aside the obvious right answer.

Vegetables grown by corporate farms that are processed and packaged, and meats encased in plastic have no taste. As a result, people lose all sense of what is fresh and good and nutritious. There is no life force left in our food sources, and yet we still settle for convenience. With all of the packaging of our food, people lose sight of how it gets to their tables. I have had kids come to our school and not know where hamburger came from. Instead of knowing that the beef came from a cow, their response when asked where it came from was McDonalds.

Modern man's desire for an easier life than his ancestor's has almost eliminated his connection with nature. Nature isn't always convenient, but we need to find balance. Our desire to conquer nature has distanced us from magic and wonder. We relate to it as if we were in a museum looking through the glass. Most people's relationship with nature is cognitive through television documentaries. We engage passively.

Coming home to the natural world is where many people long to be today. Since people have entered the so called civilized age we have done all that we can to separate ourselves from nature. We wear heavy layers of clothes so we do not feel the weather. We wear thick shoes so we do not feel the earth. We build houses and buildings that keep us from feeling, seeing and hearing nature. Throughout most of our lives we attempt to separate ourselves from nature, which causes a feeling of emptiness in our hearts and souls. We become so sheltered that we lose that sense of really being alive.

Hearing people say that their idea of camping out is in a hotel makes me sad. I feel bad that they can't release their bondage ties to material comfort and external technological stimulus for a few, life enriching days. They've detached themselves from feeling anything that's real, and should be natural for us.

Yet, with all these doomsday reports, I know how simple it would be to reverse it all. It's so simple that it's almost impossible to achieve. I truly believe that finding one's own personal connection with nature is finding one's power, and finding one's power is what creates miracles and change.

If sixty percent of Americans could find a personal connection with nature, we would more than likely affect a huge change in global warming almost instantaneously. It's like the crumbling of the Berlin Wall. When an entire culture had a paradigm shift in their perception, a divisive wall came down quickly.

I also know it's not easy these days to connect with nature, for most of the great wild areas that were accessible have been built upon in one way or another. The few natural recreation areas that we have set aside near the outskirts of suburbs and cities have lists of rules about staying on the designated paths and what you can and can't do, and where you can and can't go. There is no adventure in exploring these controlled, open spaces. It's great that those places do exist, but there is such a craving demand for that freedom of natural space that they are overcrowded. Not one minute will go by without seeing someone walking, running or riding a bike pass by, and more often than not they have a cell phone or music earphones stuck in their ears, allowing no room for anything else to come into them.

We have lost the respect and care for our earth because we no longer live in it, but upon it. Think of a time when you were moved by a sunset or felt peaceful and happy sitting quietly under a tree. Perhaps a bird migration caught your eye as you drove, sealed within your car, and you felt an inexplicable yearning.

Remember the last time you were caught in a storm and it made you feel alive, even humbled?

The more distant human beings get from nature and the earth, the greater their unhappiness seems to become.

I find I am always amazed when one of my adult students sits quietly in nature observing the minutiae of life- a spider spinning a delicate, intricate pattern between branches, or the industry of a colony of ants carrying the carcass of an insect three times their size- that they are moved to unexplained tears. Their faces become softer and they become less defensive.

These tears are usually tears of sadness for all that they've missed in their rapid paced lives, but in time those tears turn to gratitude for finally having the experience they've been unknowingly craving. They are connecting with their primal self or the "spirit that moves in all things". These men and women have been touched, some for the first time, by the earth and her slow moving rhythms. They are connecting with nature and their true selves. They finally have a feeling of truly belonging, and not feeling isolated. The frantic pace of their lives have held them captive until that moment, and they make promises to themselves to get out in nature more often when they return to their routines.

Our culture doesn't allow for those promises, and eventually, unless relentlessly pursued, most people come to doubt that the connection really existed. The cities don't allow for quiet time. Earth-connections aren't supported in most schools, and families are so busy there is barely time for family dinners once a week.

One of the greatest gifts a parent can give themselves and their child is quiet time in nature, whether it's at the beach, or in the mountains or desert or in their backyard.

Most of the kids that I work with have absolutely no ability to spend time by themselves. They don't read. They don't like to be alone. They have to be entertained from the outside in, rather than entertaining themselves from the inside out. Eyes glued to computers, and cell phones permanently attached to ears, music blaring to numb the mind, and shopping malls, acting as playgrounds, are defining the character of the next generation of our youth. It worries me of what our world will be like in twenty years as our children grow up in a world so removed from the very force that gives us life and sustains us.

We all enjoy the convenience and comfort of our warm houses and all of our toys, and we are social creatures by nature, but again, it's all about balance. Not all or nothing.

Sitting quietly in nature, observing and listening bring us into a state of presence. Daily practices, such as meditation, are tools to bring us back to the present moment. Most spiritual practices tell us that the present moment is the only moment that matters because in that present moment it is the only time that truly exists, and that's our opening where we can connect to that universal energy flow, or spirit that move in all things, and co-create and manifest whatever we choose. That I believe is what is meant when it is said that the power is now. Finding that opening is what will create change.

Sitting quietly in nature without the noise of city life, the sirens or honking of horns, without television and without the addictions of technology, can be overwhelming to those who avoid being alone. But it is in the moments of quiet observance that the answers come. Answers to why we're here, or what the next step might be, or who we are and what we might need to change. Answers come in flashes to questions we haven't even had time to sit and ask yet.

To sit quietly in nature and observe is to become part of the majesty within the simplicity of life's tasks. The ants carry the carcass to the colony to feed the colony. The spider weaves his web for food and joy. They know why they are here.

Becoming involved and being present can be both an exhilarating and painful journey. The more conscious you become of the natural world and your place in it, the more painful it is to bear witness to the losses.

We live in a society that doesn't respect nature, the earth or our finite resources. There is an ancient way of thinking that the earth and its resources are for man's exploitation, while the real kingdom exists after death. This thinking is emerging again in a conservative movement that honors corporate plunder over humanitarian concerns.

There are times when best intentions, commitment, desire and being present aren't enough to ward off feelings of hopelessness or depression. There are days when every time you pick up a newspaper there is nothing but bad news on all fronts. Those are the times that can engender cynicism and callousness. Those are the times when we lose our innocence and focus and we are willing to give up and say, "What does it matter anyway? I'm only one person." Yet, those are the times when we need to be the most vigilant to our deepest longings and desires.

I grew up in a beautiful place near a reservoir, along the tree-lined Stevens Creek, in the Santa Cruz Mountains. Below was the valley now known as the Silicon Valley, which was lush with fruit tree orchards, meandering creeks and woods. It was in a time not too long ago when you could drink pure water straight from the earth there. It was a Garden of Eden that is now congested with houses, mini-malls, apartments, computer companies, concrete and pollution.

It broke my heart every time a new road or subdivision or mini-mall was built because I had established such a deep connection with its vast natural reserves. I became angry and frightened at the same time, for if this was what was happening to my little corner of the world, I could only imagine what was happening in other parts of the country, and the world as a whole. The more I studied the more fanatical I became. I became an earth warrior ready to do battle with anyone or anything that destroyed the beauty of old-growth forests, or threatened to fill in marshland for condo projects. The angrier I became, the more depressed I became. I was spiraling out of control and out of center, and willing to do the same kind of harm to those who were harming "my earth".

It was nature, the spirit of earth who taught me to let go. The victim of all the devastation taught me that she and her beings would survive long past man's demise. A few earthquakes, disease, hurricanes, extreme storms and climate changes, that bore the extinction of animals and plants so vital to man's survival, would cleanse her surface and heal her wounds so she could start all over again. Like a dog shaking water from its fur, we would all disappear and she would continue to heal.

I personally don't believe that the spirit of earth wants that - she needs mankind as much as mankind needs her, so she is telling us a bit more forcefully to change our ways or lose them. She couldn't be more desperate at this point, but she is still hopeful and still trying to salvage her resources. So instead of becoming more fanatical, I released my anger into the earth, and I connected with her spirit on a cosmic eternal level. I try to teach others to be respectful, mindful, and to know that like our lives, it could all be temporary, unless our legacy is to insure the survival of all species, and plants, and all the glorious wild things we know to exist, but may never see.

A Native American teacher of mine once said, "We need to walk backward into the future". Living in cramped cities, apartments, gated communities and cookie cutter housing tracts, where nature is a manicured lawn and a professionally landscaped garden, devoid of any real "medicine", breeds estrangement from the natural wonders.

Walk backwards into the woods, live like we used to live-*in* the earth. Build an earth shelter, sleep in a bark tee pee, sit for a day under a cedar tree and watch the endless sky. Find your future!

"We are part of the earth and it is a part of us. The perfumed flowers are our sisters; the deer, the horse, the great eagle, these are our brothers. The rock crests, the juices of the meadows, the body heat of the pony, and man-all belong to the same family. This we know: all things are connected. Whatever befalls the earth befalls the sons of the earth. Man did not weave the web of life; he is merely a strand in it. Whatever he does to the web, he does to himself."

-Chief Sealth (Seattle)

NATURE AS PROTECTOR AND FRIEND

Chapter Two

My connection to nature carried me through some pretty rough emotional times when I was about seven years old. It was a dark time in my life when these events happened in broad daylight. We all suffer some traumas and have hard times, but it's how we handle those experiences that define our character. Do we become perpetual victims to our trauma or do we allow the experience to mold us into better, more compassionate people?

We were living in Cupertino, an All-American neighborhood, in northern California. My parents knew most of our neighbors and socialized with them frequently. I could easily ride my bike to my friend's houses to play without fear of abduction, as is unfortunately a common fear today. There was a different fear lurking in that neighborhood for me however.

We lived at the beginning of a cul-de-sac with about eight houses, each on an acre of land. "The Dark People", as I called them, lived at the end of the circle. They were ordinary looking, in their late 30's or early 40's. Mary wasn't particularly outstanding. She was attractive but not excessively so. She was lively and outgoing and very talkative. I liked her immensely for her seeming warmth and friendliness. She wore light-framed glasses, and dresses and lots of jewelry. She had dirty blond hair, cut in a longish bob.

Art was tall and thin and not very attractive. He was aloof and mysterious with a powerful presence that couldn't be ignored. He always wore blue jeans with a striped railroad type shirt. I vividly remember his steel toed, work boots because he would kick me with them. He had a thin, black moustache, like a Fu Manchu, that seemed to define his entire face. He was dark haired with bushy eyebrows, and had a perpetual smirk on his face that always sent chills down my spine.

Their son was a friend of mine who I liked to visit, not only for his company, but I also liked to visit all of their animals. They kept them in an outside shed. Some were loose and some were in cages, and I quickly learned that they weren't very happy animals. There was another shed in the yard that we weren't allowed to go into, which of course, always held a great fascination for me. Separate from that shed, there was a secret locked room off the back of the house with taped over windows. The shed and the room both exuded a dark, ominous energy that I always felt, but didn't understand.

It was an early evening in the spring when I snuck into the shed while Mary and Art were in the house. I slowly opened the door and the smell of urine and death assaulted my senses. I should have closed the door and ran, but I wanted to see what could smell so bad. As my eyes adjusted to the darkness, I saw cats and dogs tied up to the wall. I recognized one of the dogs as a neighbor's pet that had been declared lost. I saw dead animals hanging from the ceiling. It so overwhelmed my senses that my mind was spinning and reeling from the horror. As I turned to run, Art was standing behind me like a wall. He kicked me, and shoved me into the room and slammed the door so quickly that I didn't have time to react or cry out. I freaked and started to pound on the door, crying to get out of that hell, but Art had left and there was no one to rescue me. I sat on the floor trying to figure out what to do next.

As dark as the shed was, there were cracks in the single walled redwood planks, which let in little beams of light, allowing me to see the neighbor's dog and the other animals, including the dead ones. I calmed down when the neighbor's dog laid next to me licking my hand, as if to tell me it would be okay. As I petted him my eyes adjusted to the dark and I could see the other dogs and cats, some tortured and some emaciated. There was fecal matter everywhere, as well as the bones of other unidentified, dead animals. It was hell, and my seven-year-old mind couldn't understand or grasp why these neighbors, who had never harmed me until that point, could be so cruel to the animals. I felt as if the animals were communicating their feelings to me. Their pain and fear shot into me like a bolt of electricity - separate from what I was feeling. It was as if I could read their minds. I had never had this kind of feeling and it almost frightened me, but I loved animals so much that I knew I wasn't in danger from them.

I lay down with the dog and fell asleep, so I don't know how long I was kept in there, but the door opened with a force letting in a flood of light, which startled me awake. I noticed immediately the dogs and cats cowered, trying to hide in the shadows, out of sight from Art. Art grabbed my arm and yanked me outside. He knelt down at eye level with me and the look in his eyes terrified me. They were cold and seemed to be pure black, lacking any life force. He told me to never tell anyone what I saw in there, and if I did he would kill my cat and dog or worse. Bizarrely, he then took me into his kitchen for a snack, as if nothing had happened. I thought for a moment that perhaps it was a nightmare that hadn't actually happened, but as I left the house to go home the reality of it sunk in and I began to plot how I would rescue the animals. It became everything to me.

Art and Mary had instilled such a fear in me with their threats against my animals and my family that I didn't tell anyone. It confused me that adults could be so cruel to animals. They were killing and torturing innocent beings, while holding them captive without food or water for long periods of time.

I kept going back because I thought I could save some of the animals. A couple of times I did sneak to the shed when they were in their house and opened the door to free as many animals as I could. When they caught me, they would lock me in the shed. Sometimes they would beat me, and sometimes they would cut me on parts of my body where the marks didn't show. This went on for about two years. I think those horrible people tried to convert me to their satanic ways. They saw how I related to the animals, and how I had the ability to communicate with them on a different level. They wanted to use that gift in their life-ending rituals.

There were other horrors in that shed, memories that even today I choose not to access. Yet, I knew even at such a young age, that they would have minimal impact on me. My bond with the animals was so much stronger than their sickness. Whenever Art and Mary locked me in the shed, the animals would comfort me. We would lie together in the dark, cuddling each other. Sometimes they would even lie on top of me as if I were part of their four-legged pack. It was a magical thing amidst the terror. I was constantly making trouble for those people, which helped me from being emotionally taken over by them. My greatest comfort and solace always came from nature. I would spend hours next to one of my sacred trees. I felt protected by it, and I felt that its strength gave me strength.

How does a child make sense of that evil and remain relatively unscathed as he or she grows? I know now, as an adult, that adversity and tragedy can either doom us to live guarded, defensive lives or create an opening that makes us stronger and wiser. Often when siblings share a dire circumstance, one grows from it and the other shuts down. Why does one prosper and the other not? I'm not sure of that answer, but I do know that the dark place gave me one of the biggest gifts of my life.

During one of the beatings, as I was lying on the floor of the shed, I found my spirit traveling to another place, another dimension. My body was being hurt, but my mind was traveling into another realm, a place just as real and vibrant as the physical world. As I was drifting through a gauze-like veil into a meadow, exploding with the lavender, yellow and red of wildflowers, a huge 1,500-pound grizzly bear came to greet me. He nuzzled me and I felt completely safe. I was so happy to be with him that I wrapped myself around him, burying my face and as much of my body as I could in his fur. He smelled of berries and dirt. His fur was coarse and warm and he played with me until my hurts disappeared. He let me know that he would always be in that realm for me, and that I could go to him whenever I wanted or needed him.

Decades later he is still with me. He is my spirit animal, my protector and my savior. Much later in life I became acquainted with the terminology spirit world and spirit guide; yet, as a child I didn't need to know the words. I naturally accessed a world that not only took me deeper into the primal mysteries of our physical world, but a world that saved my emotional life.

I had been mentored since I was five years old in the ways of the woods by an old, Italian man who had lived near us, so I knew my territory well. It was as much my home as the house I lived in. I would often sneak out of my house at night, even at that young age with no fear, to spend as much time as I could in the woods behind our house. There was an irresistible pull, particularly to an old, giant, oak tree full of knotholes and twisting branches. It was my grandfather. I called it Grandfather Oak, and its mighty branches and leaves absorbed me into its mystery. At night it looked as if it had a mouth that was speaking to me. It might have been scary to most kids, but to me it was welcoming and comforting. I would wrap my arms around its trunk and I felt that it actually loved me. The oak's energy calmed me and gave me strength, and protected me during those fearful times - a communication we shared for years.

Grandfather Oak was one of the first non-humans that taught me about communicating and bonding with other non-humans. In synchronous harmony with the caged animals in the shed, I learned how each living being has a feeling tone and energy that can be sensed and shared. It's easier when one is young and still unformed by adult perceptions of what is supposedly real, but it is not a gift just for children. Adults can communicate in that manner as well if they simply change their perception and re-examine their belief system.

I decided that I would set up a camp at the base of my new friend. I made a simple stick shelter, up against a log at the tree's base, and covered it with leaves and other forest litter. Unbeknownst to my parents, I would spend nights there and I gradually became a part of that place. In time the animals began to show themselves to me, as I was no longer an outsider. Being a child, my energies were pure and non-threatening, and I was open to receiving the blessings that the natural world can bestow.

I remember one night quickly falling asleep, exhausted from the fear that I had experienced during the day. I was awakened with a start in the middle of the night by something touching me. When I looked I discovered a raccoon was making his bed at the foot of my blanket. It was if my dog had shown up and I remember saying, "Where have you been all this time?" I didn't try to touch him, as I knew that he was still a wild animal and I respected his power. He snuffled and curled into a ball and went to sleep, as did I.

The next night my raccoon friend returned again and curled up at the foot of my blanket, but this time he let me touch him. He didn't come back for a long time however, and I missed his comforting presence at night. When he did return, we got to know each other well. He never tried to bite me or hurt me in any way; in fact, he often stayed with me for long periods of time. I think that was my first experience really understanding the meaning of the word sacred. There was no other word for the bond that the raccoon and I had.

There were many other wondrous moments as well. I woke one morning to find six deer sleeping around me, the closest just five feet or so away. When I got up they didn't run, but seemed content to let me do my thing.

I began to spend more time among the branches of my Grandfather Oak, more time in fact than on the ground. I gathered sticks and carefully built a lean-to shelter in the branches, with my neighbor the squirrel just above me. Above the squirrel and I was a hawk's nest. The branches were so thick and lush that the squirrel was never in danger from the hawk, and the hawk never felt threatened by my presence.

Eventually my lean-to grew into a hut about six-by-six foot square, where I could sleep comfortably. I was like a bird in its nest, high among the branches, safe from predators. I was so well hidden that one day two men walking in my direction didn't see me, as they took no care to fit into the natural flow of the woods. Because of my experiences with the "dark people" I was distrustful. I got a weird feeling about these two men so I kept very quiet. They stopped to talk for what seemed like an eternity right underneath me. My heart was pounding so hard that I wondered if they could hear it. I asked the tree to help me stay calm, and I wrapped my arms around a branch and let my heart beat into the tree. Amazingly, the tree seemed to take the fear from me. Eventually the men moved on and they never looked up to see me there.

My childish eyes saw Grandfather Oak and Big Bear as individual friends and protectors. Even today, I see trees and plants and animals as individuals, not as groups. When I walk through the woods I feel a communication with the trees or specific plants, and I often will spend time in silent union with one that I am particularly drawn to.

Unlike humans, the oak and raccoon, the deer and Big Bear were my guides and solace during the time of the dark people. Perhaps because of my youth and my openness to the spirit energies of the non-human world, and the emotional trauma that I was suffering, I was able to connect deeply with the natural world, and gratefully, that sense of safety and belonging has never left me.

I believe that most children, who are lucky enough to have had that connection in childhood, but let it go as they grow, always seem to have a vague yearning and emptiness as adults. They are unaware that their youthful connection can be rekindled.

A child doesn't have to be Henry David Thoreau before he or she begins to connect with nature. Learning about the woods and acquiring the skills of a woodsman helps to establish and deepen that connection. A local park or preserve is an excellent place to start, and the woods themselves will begin to teach. Finding a quiet spot and simply listening can be revelatory for those who are always rushed and have deadlines.

Nature is easier for kids to connect with than for adults, as they are purer, their hearts are open and their minds not yet bound by cultural conformities. The key to making any kind of connection with nature is to have an open heart, which is hard for some adults who have built up defensive walls. I tell all my students to listen with their entire bodies not just their ears, and to see with their entire bodies, not just their eyes. The deeper connections don't happen in the brain. The deeper connections happen first in the heart and in the gut. It's the same with having a deep connection with another person. The eyes may initially attract you, but it's your intuition and heart that take you deeper.

The intuitive hunch is also about trusting - trusting that what you feel is real. All people are intuitive. It's one of God's or Spirit's protective gifts to mankind. It's learning to trust our intuition that takes time and practice, particularly when we are all so busy and distracted. Some people call it the sixth sense or inner vision. It's that inner vision that can connect you with all the wonders of life and protect you from the negative forces.

There are many things in nature that we feel or maybe even see, but can't explain. Nature spirits are a mystery. The logical mind refutes their existence, but the part of you that is soul and spirit know they are everywhere. When we spend some quality time outdoors – quality time is without electronics or daily to-do lists – the extraneous baggage of our life washes away and we are left with our true selves. That thought scares a lot of people because sometimes there isn't much of a *true* self. It wasn't developed or allowed to create itself. Instead of being overtaken by the fear, start developing and creating a new you. Some people just won't be able to tolerate the empty space, which isn't really empty, but those who do will begin to have a new relationship, not only with themselves, but the world around them.

I talk a lot about dirt time. This is the essence of what I teach. It is the time that a person spends in the woods or anywhere in nature by their selves perfecting their outdoor skills and becoming as comfortable outside as one is inside.

A great starting place is with a tree. If you are standing at the edge of a forest or even in the midst of hundreds of trees, ask yourself if there is a particular tree that seems to call to you. If you feel something, trust it. Go with it. Go to the tree and hug it, bury your face in the bark and smell its earthiness, climb it and sit in the branches. Really look at the tree, look at its beauty. Talk to it, cry on its trunk and ask for its help. Observe the insects that crawl on its bark-skin. Make a bed under your tree and camp there overnight. Your tree, like my Grandfather Oak, will take care of you. It will calm you and give you an inner peace you might have never felt until then. Let yourself be open to everything going on near you – the sounds, the smells and your thoughts. Maybe you will even be lucky enough to see the nature spirits – the "little people".

My nights spent with Grandfather Oak opened up my senses to all kinds of things. I began to see earth spirits or what are known as divas. I'd watch them floating through the air. They were different shapes and sizes and sometimes just little pieces of light. Sometimes they looked like a little person. Because I was a kid I never thought any of this was strange. I thought it was just part of being in the woods. As an adult I have found that many people, particularly gardeners and others who spend a lot of time in nature, see these beings as well.

Another way to connect deeply in nature and with your favorite tree is to climb it and sit among its branches. I used to sit up high in my oak with my buddy the squirrel, just a few branches above me, and feel the power of the tree. I could even feel the water being sucked up from the roots. It was an incredible sensation and I felt as if I were part of the tree. I would sometimes close my eyes and visualize myself going into the tree and traveling through its bark layers. I later learned that there is a name for that way of connecting. It is an exercise called "grokking".

A full-grown tree is one of the most powerful beings in nature. It bears the power of high winds and storms, swaying with the gusts as if it were dancing. The roots of the tree spread deep under ground some 50 to 100 feet, stabilizing it as it grows. It stands majestically in one spot for the entirety of its life, watching over all the creatures that live in its branches or in its bark. If you sit in your tree for any length of time you will feel the quiet majesty of your new friend. I think trees are happy when people explore them and touch them.

I remember trees, like some people remember childhood friends. I figure I was about 10 years old and I was doing my usual exploring in the woods, when I heard noises that sounded like rocks being thrown against rocks. It seemed to trigger something inside me because I got a sick feeling in my gut, and I knew something was wrong. The noises were coming from the creek where I had a small brush shelter, so I quietly and quickly made my way there. I slowed into a stealthy movement called a "stalk" to close the gap between the noise and me.

When I got close, I looked out from behind a thick, coffee berry bush and saw three boys about my own age, throwing rocks at something. As I focused my sight, I could see that they were throwing rocks at lizards that were sunning themselves on the river rocks along the streambed. They were beautiful swifts, or blue bellies, as we used to call them, and I could see that the boys had managed to kill one of them. I crawled closer through a patch of stinging nettle, taking care not to be seen or heard until I reached the edge of the creek, where I could see the poor, dead lizard.

I wasn't particularly big for my age, and these boys were a bit older and bigger, and well-known bullies at my school, but when I saw what they were doing my Big Bear inner power welled up in me and filled me with an intense need to protect the lizards. I leapt to my feet screaming at the boys to stop. Unfortunately, my Big Bear power had no effect on them, and they just laughed at me and continued to stone the lizards. I was so mad, however, that I picked up a stick and threw it at them, hitting one of the kids, which only made the matter worse. I tried to talk my way out of the inevitable confrontation as they began to circle up on me. I knew I was out-numbered, and I bolted like a frightened deer running toward the creek, hopping and leaping over rocks and boulders, splashing through water and clambering over downed, tree trunks. I was ahead of them, but it wasn't going to be easy to get away from those young, athletic boys intent on getting me. I felt like I was running for my life. I had seen these kids gang up on someone else before and I knew I was in big trouble.

I ran a gauntlet down the stream, when I suddenly felt like I was being pulled, almost as if someone had reached out and grabbed me by the shirt. My heart was pounding, and when I turned to look there was no one there. It occurred to me that I was feeling the pulling in my gut. I stepped toward the pulling sensation and I was literally yanked into a giant, old oak, much like Grandfather Oak. I was in a notch of the tree. It was as if the tree had pulled me into it. The bullies soon caught up but ran past me. I felt safe there just as I did in my Grandfather Oak. When the boys ran past, I climbed into the higher branches of the tree, knowing that they would head back that way when they didn't find me. Once again, when they did come back they never saw me in the tree. It proved to me yet again that nature can be a great friend and protector. It's always there, the door that never closes, the friend who is always available.

"Life outside a person is an extension of the life within him. This compels him to be a part of it and accept responsibility for all creatures great and small. Life becomes harder when we live for others, but it also becomes richer and happier."
-Albert Schweitzer

"It is not the critic who counts; not the one who points out how the strong stumbled, or where the doer of deeds cold have done better. The credit belongs to the one who is actually in the arena; whose face is marred by dust and sweat and blood; who strives valiantly; who errs and comes up short again and again; who knows great enthusiasm and great devotion; who spends him/herself in a worthy cause; who at best knows in the end the triumph of high achievement and who, at the worst, if he/she fails, at least fails while daring greatly, so that his/her place shall never be with those timid souls who know neither victory nor defeat."

-Theodore Roosevelt

PROTECTING NATURE

Chapter Three

Why should we protect nature and what does it mean to do so? The earth will most likely be here long after mankind has disappeared. Man may just be the primary hand in his own demise. If we are not conscious of our abuse to a finite resource, that resource can and most likely will retaliate with all its force and power to destroy all the things we take for granted. Earthquakes, floods and droughts have proven how fragile our infrastructures are in their mighty wake.

My primal, protector self emerged in such a way that made me want to protect this earth and her living, non-verbal beings when I was quite young. I grew up in a beautiful place where the Santa Cruz Mountains meet the Santa Clara Valley, now known as the Silicon Valley.

There are many places today whose beauty has succumbed to man's insatiable need to develop and build. When I grew up, the Valley was a riparian woodland with tall and commanding oaks, redwood forests, layered with madrones and gorgeous grasslands. In the lowlands there were orchard upon orchard of cherry, apricot, pear and a variety of other fruit trees. Like so many places, the orchards disappeared and were replaced with industrial tracts. The hillsides vanished under the sprawl of housing developments. Whenever I saw a "For Sale" sign, I knew that property was doomed. My friends and I would take the signs down and shred them to bits hoping the buyers and sellers would go away. Though we must have taken down hundreds of signs in a desperate attempt to save our forests and orchards, it was to no avail.

One of the great joys of my childhood was spending time with my beloved Uncle Bill at his home in the Colorado Rockies. Uncle Bill was over 200 pounds, big as a bear and just as scruffy. His mouth was curled up on the ends because he spent so much time laughing, and he loved nature more than any other person I knew.

His backyard was a nature wonderland. There were aspen thickets flocked with singing birds, crystal-clear, water pools filled with fish, and mountain vistas carpeted with some of the most beautiful wildflowers my young eyes had ever seen.

Uncle Bill taught me so much about nature, but he also gave me one of the greatest teachings of my life. I remember a conversation where he asked me what I was willing to die for. Although I was only 11 year olds and thought I would live forever, and wondered why I would need to die for anything, I respected everything Uncle Bill said to me, so I took this question quite seriously. He explained that being willing to die for something commits you to life. As we talked, I told him that I would die for my parents, for him, to protect myself, and I also said that

I would be willing to die for the Earth. At such a young age, I don't think I appreciated the gravity of the question, nor the gravity of my answer, but it resonated to the deepest parts of me then, and it continues to resonate within me as an adult.

When I returned home at the end of my summer visit, bulldozers were destroying one of my sacred spots. The forest and hillsides had been my stomping ground, where I had made trails and built a fort, where I hunted and fished, watched snakes, where I could sit for hours just watching nature unfold, where I felt safe. My home for the past four years was going to be destroyed and there was nothing I could do about it. I would sneak close to the worksite and watch as the huge trucks rumbled past. In grief and amazement, I watched the men in the trucks destroy a world so full of life with so little regard. They excavated and hauled, and dumped load after load of precious earth to mine sand to make concrete for roads and buildings.

One day after school, when I was heading for my Grandfather Oak, I found a chain-link fence wrapped all around it and a sign on the facing declaring, "No Trespassing". There were red, surveyor's flags around the tree and paint marks on its trunk. I watched as a man with a chainsaw started to cut the limbs and sections from the tree and began to load it into a big truck. He was destroying Grandfather Oak. He was killing one of my dearest friends. I remember screaming at the man, and charging him with tears running down my face, but I couldn't stop him. He just yelled back and pushed me away. I kept charging and screaming and suddenly found there were three men who grabbed me, and threw me outside the fenced enclosure and locked the gate. I gave up at that point and had to watch brokenheartedly, as they methodically reduced Grandfather Oak down from its full, branched-out majesty to a mere stump. It was literally as if they were cutting a vital organ from my body.

When the workers left, I went to what was remaining of my protector and friend – a two foot stump. All I could do was sit on the stump and cry my eyes out. These were men who only saw it as firewood, and not a child's living, treasured friend. Grandfather

Oak had protected me in my darkest hours of childhood, and I was powerless to protect it in return.

Not only did they cut my friend down, but countless other trees as well. Some were butchered to create more sunlight for the inevitable sprawl of houses to come. Sometimes the developers would spare a handful of oak trees, only to lay pavement around them, which ultimately killed them. Even as a kid, I knew that oak trees spread their roots out underground in a large area to collect the water that falls in California's short, rainy season. The cement poured so close to the trunk prevents the water from soaking into the ground and the trees die. I remember trying to explain this to the builders who looked at me as if I were an alien.

Society in general tends to overlook the untainted wisdom of children, when that obvious truth isn't convenient or profitable. Later in life, as an adult, I was taken more seriously and I was able to have a greater impact on the builders of a subdivision in Scotts Valley called, appropriately enough, "The Oaks". They listened, and created another solution for the trees. By leaving a bigger space around the trees, and spacing brick before the edge of the cement sidewalk, it allowed for more movement with growth, and provided space between the bricks to allow rain seepage to water the roots.

I would often return during the year to sit on the stump and be with my fallen friend. I could sometimes still see the tree in all its glory and feel its wonderful energy. Its presence had been so powerful through all its years that some vestige of it still existed, and that feeling comforted me. I like to think that my presence gave comfort to its spirit as well.

The loss of my sacred spot overwhelmed me. I kept hearing Uncle Bill's question in my mind over and over. Was I willing to die for my sacred spot? I thought so, but all I could really do was watch them destroy what I held so dear. I vowed to never just watch again. I would defend the earth and animals as best I could.

As civilization encroached more and more upon that spot, the spirit of the tree was soon gone and my time of grieving had passed. I learned a vital lesson from Grandfather Oak and from the woods, which was that nature not only protects those who go to her with open hearts, but that nature needs to be protected as well.

It's part of the Gaia principle. The earth body has its own soul from which springs all life, including man. Our inner spirit and the inner spirit of the earth are interconnected. All plants, and animals, and insects, and stones, and mountains, and rivers, and oceans know this, and know their unique positions within this reality. Human beings seem to be the only species that tries to negate this interconnectedness by destroying the very source that gives him life.

Already having an innate knowing of this principle, and as a result of my passionate need to defend nature, I became known at school as the "Nature Freak". While most kids were playing sports, I was in the woods. Kids could be as cruel then as they can be now and they would chant, "Nature Freak" over and over when they saw me. Yet, I took that name seriously. I was a nature freak and proud of it.

Once, I caught a boy trying to burn a nest of baby robins by pouring kerosene on them and setting them on fire. My primal self emerged. I was enraged and I chased that kid for blocks with the intent of beating him senseless. I didn't catch him, but I felt the courage of my conviction – to defend. When I returned to the nest to hopefully save the young lives, I found four, charred, little bodies. My heart broke at the sound of the mother chirping madly from the tree branch above.

That incident was not an isolated case. I remember cats and dogs being teased and hurt by people. The wanton killing of animals seemed common, even among my peers. It was very confusing for me, as I could never consciously hurt an animal, even a small, unusual creature.

On a hike in the Santa Cruz Mountains with a friend, we came upon a beautiful, banana slug. My friend started pouring salt on it, which is a terrible way for a banana slug to die, as it sucks the moisture from it. I couldn't believe that my friend could be so cruel and before I could think I slugged him. My instincts again emerged to defend. It might sound silly to get so upset over a banana slug, but to me that lump of yellow was as important to defend as the larger creatures, and maybe even more so. I felt bad about hitting my friend, but he never hurt another creature again.

In middle school, I learned another important lesson about how our society views cruelty to animals, and the consequences or lack of consequences. I was on the wharf at the Santa Cruz beach where people like to fish and watch the birds. I saw a guy baiting his hook with a fish so he could catch a pelican. He swung the fish into the water and a pelican dove and caught it. The guy started reeling it in, flying the pelican like a kite for a couple of seconds until the line broke. I told some bystanders and an employee at the wharf what I had seen and we confronted the man. Someone else had called the police, who talked to the idiot, but were powerless to do anything more. It was heartening to see that people cared, but disheartening to find out the consequences for such cruelty were non-existent. I wondered if the kid who burned the robins or the fool who tortured the pelican for his own amusement felt remorse when confronted.

Remorse is a great educator. Remorse gave me an understanding of what I committed my life to. Even though I was a nature freak and I had vowed to never consciously hurt an animal, I still had my own lessons to learn.

I experienced one of life's great, defining moments when I was playing football with a bunch of friends on a grass field at school. Dozens of gulls were flying around us, and like any primal, non-thinking kid with a stick or a rock or a football, I threw that ball as hard as I could at one of the birds. I never thought I would hit it. I was showing off and I hit one of the gulls square and it tumbled from the sky. It flopped around sideways with one of its wings useless and hanging limp. I was horror struck by what I had done and I felt physically sick. All the other kids scattered, knowing I had done something bad. I was scared but I couldn't run.

I learned that I wasn't immune to getting caught up in the gang mentality of wanting to fit in, without thinking about cause and affect. That all important pause button to think of consequences wasn't there.

I went to the gull and sat close by watching it writhing in pain. It tried to get away from me but couldn't. It looked me in the eye seeming to ask why I had done such a thing. I felt that bird's pain. I moved closer and eventually got close enough to pick it up and hold it in my arms. I knew I had made a mistake that I couldn't fix. I had caused a living creature pain and I sobbed for the bird, and I cried for me. I tried to give it my loving energy, like the animals gave to me during the "dark days", but the wing was broken and my loving energy wasn't enough. When the animal-care authorities arrived they looked at the bird and simply said it needed to be put to sleep to spare it the pain.

While I had been holding the bird, looking into its eyes and begging it to forgive me, something happened deep within me. I had a felt knowing through that experience, of what I would die for, what I would commit myself to. I knew that for the rest of my life whenever or wherever help was needed to protect nature or animals I would do it. It wasn't just an idea any longer. The gull taught me about respect for life.

Soon after that day I was able to stand by that conviction, in a small, but defining way. My dad and I were going to film the pollution that washed up on Franklin Point beach, near where we lived. Franklin Point is an incredibly beautiful place with acres of rolling, sand dunes, marshes, willow thickets, wildflowers, tide pools and abundant wild life. Amongst this beauty is the garbage that washes onto the beach from boats dumping their waste further out in the ocean.

While I was shooting the film, we came across an injured, beached seal. About that time a man and his dogs were coming from the opposite direction from us. He let his dogs loose and they surrounded the seal trying to attack it. My father was a fairly passive man who didn't like to get involved in situations like this, but I was not. My protective instincts exploded and I ran for the dogs yelling. I looked them in the eye, and I am sure they saw one crazy son of a bitch, and they actually backed off. I lit into their owner telling him that seals were my friends and his stupidity or pathetic pleasure at watching his dogs torture a seal was unconscionable and sick. He started to say something, but saw that wild rage in my eyes and turned and walked away. We waited for a while to make sure the seal was safe and continued to film along the beach a ways. When I came back, the seal had moved into the surf, at least momentarily safe from moronic humans.

Being true to one's beliefs is hard. It takes work and commitment. It's much easier to sit on the sidelines and let others act. Because our lives become so busy with daily routines and obligations, there is little time at the end of the day to connect meaningfully with others, let alone ourselves. Many people don't even know what they believe in. They rely on other's thoughts through groups or organizations and peer pressure to define who they are.

There were a few incidences that shaped my view of the world in a negative way. From them I had to learn that sometimes you just have to be at peace with a situation that you can't fix. Sometimes fear gets in the way and sometimes you don't know how to fix it.

One incident happened when I was a young teenager. My friend Mark, who was a hiking buddy and a good friend, had a terrible home life. His father was a cruel, authoritarian man who took pleasure in beating his wife and kids. He didn't even care that I was around at times when he took his wrath out on his wife. Mark and I would cower in his room, too afraid to do anything, and too confused by his dad's behavior.

His father took us on a fishing trip to Lake Tahoe, where the water is so cold and clear it seems that you can see eternity in its depths. He was having trouble with the boat motor and topped it off with oil, then dumped the half full bottle in the lake. Mark and I were horrified, but we just looked at each other in shock, too afraid of his dad to say a word.

Mark's dad was also a landlord and accumulated lots of old appliances. He used to dump washing machines and dryers off the cliffs in the Santa Cruz Mountains. Mark and I were actually able to have some impact on that though. We would find out where he dumped them, then hauled the old machines into the back of the truck and took them to the dump without his dad ever knowing.

Another incident, I remember as vividly today as the day it happened. I was able to spend a couple of summers working with an old horse packer who led trips in the Trinity Alps Wilderness in northern California. Blackie came right from central casting. He was a tough cowboy with leathered skin from years of working outdoors. He knew the wilderness like we know our neighborhoods. I was able to learn many wilderness skills from him in some of the most remote country in the United States. It was heaven for a nature freak like me to spend time with Blackie and his beloved dog Blue.

Blue was a mutt, part Australian shepherd and part who knows what, with the personality of a stand-up comic. He made me laugh and we bonded immediately. He would crawl in my sleeping bag at night and I would put my feet on him. Most dogs are the bed warmers, but not Blue. He crawled in with me to keep *himself* warm. He would shiver until my feet surrounded him. He was a good trail dog, always watchful of the horses with a keen eye to what was happening along the trail.

One day as Blackie, Blue and I were walking the trail alongside of our horses, a fawn ambled from the woods into an open meadow. Blue took off like a shot and chased the terrified fawn out of our sight. Neither Blackie nor I had ever seen Blue do that so we were momentarily dumbstruck. The quickest way to give chase was on horseback and when we finally caught up to Blue he had mauled the fawn. Though still alive, she was bleeding from her haunches, gasping for the final breaths, her eyes terrified. It seemed like Blue had become a wild animal. We had to restrain him from doing more damage. Once Blue was under control, I held the fawn in my arms. We could hear the agitated stomping of hooves in the dry leaves, presuming that the fawn's mother had chased after Blue to defend her baby. Though I could barely see through my tears, the fawn's eyes and soul met my own as she let go of her short life.

It was one of the saddest experiences I had had, and I held onto that fawn hoping that I could bring her back, when the sound of the gunshot startled me. It was so close. I leapt to my feet and ran to Blackie wondering who had fired the gun, only to find Blue the receiver of the bullet. It was almost more than I could bear as I yelled at Blackie, "How could you do this?" All I could do was hold the little dog that had become a friend, while looking at the damage he had wreaked.

There was no discussion about killing Blue in Blackie's mind. Even though he had loved that dog, he said that once a dog goes wild and gets the taste of blood he has to be put down or he will keep doing it. He said it was hard but it was the "woods way". I wanted to hit Blackie, yet I also trusted and respected him. To have so many conflicting emotions and grief overwhelmed me.

That day I lost some of my innocence, and it took years to understand that the reality of such events are what toughened me to life's tragedies and inequities, but that I didn't have to become callous and cold. It takes courage to keep an open heart and open mind as nature unfolds in mysterious ways.

There is something so vile about people doing harm to nature and animals. Each time I see a cruel act I feel violent towards the person causing it, but all that does is perpetuate the harm and cruelty. People ask me how I feel about nature's cruelty – natural fires that destroy habitat and life, or animals killing each other. I am reminded of an incredible scene I witnessed in Yellowstone in winter, when a pack of wolves had surrounded an elk and were literally eating it alive. The elk brought to its knees, had surrendered to the pack, and though horrifying to hear its screams, I understood the laws of nature provide the balance. The wolves needed to eat for their survival as well.

Unlike Nature, mankind knows very little about balance. We take more than we need. We don't replenish what we take. We cast off the excess of what we didn't need in the first place. In nature everything is in perfect harmony and balance. Nothing is wasted. There is no excess among animals. Even though there are horrifying things in nature, they are in perfect balance with what is needed.

With an Irish temper and a bombastic nature, I need a calming influence to keep myself in balance. Some people turn to drugs and alcohol to numb their selves, some need technology as a companion, and some move so fast they don't and can't think. I go to the woods.

There is a mystery and a spirit in the forests that lifts me out of my crazy humanness, and connects me with the primordial energy that is the "spirit that moves in all things". Connecting with that universal spirit is what I think Joseph Campbell meant by following your "bliss". It's a place where you know you belong in harmony with all things and are in harmony with all things. I suppose artists, poets and musicians feel that place when they create. But that feeling isn't exclusive to artistic, creative people. All of us can feel it, and one of the best places to connect with it is in a quiet spot in nature. For that reason alone we should be defending our wild lands and our wild animals.

People often ask, "How can one person really make a difference?" It's done in many ways: recycling, planting trees, joining environmental groups or just being vigilant to the smaller things. Don't kill things that get into your house or car. Free them.

One of my proudest accomplishments as a boy happened when I helped some neighbors get rid of their bats. They lived in an old Victorian and were troubled by many bats in their "belfry" so to speak. They were going to call an exterminator, but I convinced them to give me a couple of days to figure out where they were getting in and out.

They had an attic with a small opening that I had to squeeze through to get into the dark space, which was the bat cave. The smell of bat guano was intense. It was like ammonia and vinegar being blown up my nose and it actually dazed me. Once I got used to the odor, I was able to stand up and turn on my flashlight to see seemingly millions of bats hanging upside-down from the ceiling, with bat guano stacked almost two feet high in places.

I figured that I had to observe them leaving from the outside, so I found a good observation point and waited for dusk when I knew they would fly out on their nocturnal journeys. Sure enough in the fading light, I heard the humming of wings and was shown a visual spectacle that awed and excited me - hundreds of the creatures flying from a hole in the roof like an explosion of black smoke. I was then able to climb a ladder to the roof and make my way to the edge, where under the eave the hole could be wired over. Although the bats had to find a new home, it was certainly a better option than the exterminator. I was a kid, I was one person, but I saved hundreds of bats from extinction because I took the time to do so.

Another example of how to protect nature is through the power of a photograph. In 1970, the year of the first Earth Day, we were studying the affects of pollution in school. A photo in *Life Magazine* showing a city shrouded in smog practically made me choke to look at it. But that photo is still embedded in my memory and was a catalyst for me to become a nature photographer. Another powerful picture was of a pile of dead, bald and golden eagles on a ranch in Wyoming found by game wardens. Ranchers in helicopters had blown 500 birds out of the sky proclaiming they were killing their sheep.

There is a book of photographs called *The Place No One Knew* by Eliot Porter, of a sacred Navajo place, where petroglyphs etched by ancient hands are submerged under a man-made lake, known as Lake Powell. The place is Glen Canyon, a place that I had visited with my Uncle before the deluge. It took seventeen years for Glen Canyon to fill up with water, and now the damn for which the beauty of the canyon was destroyed, is filling up with silt and becoming useless. It leaks so badly that Salt Lake City would have enough water for three years from the seepage. There is talk of getting rid of the damn, which I hope happens, as the sadness of what happened to that beautiful canyon still causes a deep sadness within me.

I am moved by photographs of both the beauty and the destruction of nature, as there is so much to learn from both.

Photography is not only one of the most fulfilling parts of my life, it has made me a keen observer of the natural world and deepened my relationship with it.

Unfortunately, we tend to respond very slowly to situations that we know need our attention. If something in our environment is out of balance, but doesn't show an immediate result in our daily, personal life directly, we disregard the importance and validity of our actions, and non-actions, until it's too late. We don't make inconvenient changes until it hurts bad enough. Doing the right thing isn't always convenient, but it's the right thing.

We shouldn't have to think about protecting our resources. Nature should be valued more than our cars, houses, computers etc. It's as important as breathing, and I try to instill in my students, both adults and kids, to become stewards of the land and protectors of the earth in any way they are able. One of my strongest beliefs is that we are here to be caretakers, to be of service to our environment, and to also maintain balance. Humans have been given the gift to be able to create. If we use that ability consciously great things can be achieved.

> *"Strange that man should make up lists of living things in danger, why he fails to list himself is really even stranger."*
> *-Henry Gibson*

"Everybody can be great, because anybody can serve. You don't have to have a college degree to serve. You don't have to make sure your subject and your verb agree ..to serve. You don't have to know about Plato and Aristotle to serve. You don't have to know Einstein's theory of relativity to serve. You only need a heart full of grace. A soul generated by love."
                                        -Martin Luther King Jr.

MENTORS AND TEACHERS

Chapter Four

As I got older, instead of losing that feeling of interconnection with everything, my childhood mentors and teachers rooted that innate knowing in my psyche. Indigenous cultures revered their elders, for they were the people who had survived the hardships, and who had the knowledge to help the tribe survive. A tribe or community couldn't make it without their elders to guide them to hunting grounds, or to spring meadows filled with edible plants, or to teach them about the medicinal plants. Their knowledge was passed from one generation to the next and was sought out and respected by the younger generation. Today, the older we get the less valuable we become to the next generation. Today, it's all about youth and hard bodies and very little wisdom, which comes with slowing down, persistent experience, listening and patience.

A true mentor is an adult who develops a special relationship with a child, who teaches the child skills, and creates a sense of wonder about the world. Someone who helps the child develop a sense of honor and knowledge of right and wrong. The Australians have a saying, "No rules mate, just right." which means that people don't need the rules because they should do the right thing naturally. It may sound idealistic, but I believe you have to set high goals.

A mentorship can last for years or even a lifetime; even a brief encounter with a child can have a tremendous impact that can affect the child all his or her life. Mentoring isn't just about what an adult says, but it's the energy, or a person's "juice", shared with a child that makes a difference. That energy can affect a child just by being in the mentor's presence, and it's vital for the mentor/adult to understand that the child is picking up that energy by watching and listening, observing and ultimately by imitating that adult. In essence, mentoring is a sacred trust.

I was fortunate enough to have many mentors, many adults who took the time to teach me about nature, and ultimately about life. My earliest recollection of an adult who taught me outside the realm of my family, was from an elderly man, who I remember as having wild, bright, white hair, a big nose and intense, dark, brown eyes. His face was a weathered, road map of wrinkles from long years in the sun.

I was about five years old and we lived on a farm near San Diego, with lots of prickly pear cacti surrounding our yard. The old man had gotten permission from my father to collect the cactus so he could make wine. I don't recall what exactly attracted me so much to him, perhaps it was his patience in answering every question I had, and I bombarded him with hundreds. He made me feel safe and he seemed to welcome my company and nurtured my curiosity, not only about the cactus, but with other plants as well. He didn't simply show or tell me about things, but he allowed me to get my hands on the plants and to experience things first hand. My parents trusted him enough as well to leave me in his care without worrying.

The first plant he taught me was the prickly pear. He showed me how to rub the outside of the fruit with a rock to remove all the stickers. Once removed, I could cut the fruit in half, scoop out the center and enjoy its delicious taste. The fruit was sweet and had a beautiful red color, and smelled like a watermelon. He showed me how to slice and cook the cactus pads, or nopalitos, and he helped me prepare a meal of them for my family. He showed me how slicing the pads and rubbing the juicy flesh on my skin could relieve sunburn, which was wonderful for a fair haired and light, skinned Irish boy. He told me that the plant could be put onto wounds and snakebites to help heal them as well.

By sharing his time and experience, an incredible doorway into nature was opened for me. I learned all about the wild plants growing around me. He taught me some of the most common plants, such as dandelion and sow thistle, which I brought home to my mother to include in our dinner salads. His generous spirit and teachings have stayed with me all my life. I now teach edible and useful plant classes in the hope of opening the door of the plant world to others, as he did for me. We eventually moved away from the farm and I never saw that old gentleman again, but his spirit is deeply rooted in my life and will always be a part of me.

I realize how my own experiences with children can count in a lasting way, and I try my best to give the children I teach positive experiences to remember. That man positively reinforced my thirst for seeking knowledge outside my family. As a result, I value the knowledge of elders to this day, and I try to advise young people to do the same.

In Indian and Celtic traditions, as with most indigenous cultures, the elders are the most respected people. They are the ones with knowledge and wisdom of experience. Today our mentors are television sets and computers and video games. It is rare today for a youngster to seek out training from an elder. Although, a 14-year-old boy named Chris, who I have worked with at the school, told me that he sought a master knife maker to apprentice with.

Chris had a passion for knives and knife making, and he appreciated that good knife-making was an art form. Chris told me that when he asked the man to teach him, the man actually cried because he was sure that his trade would disappear. By 18, he was well on his way to making not just functional knives, but the works of art he appreciated at age 14. Chris had a calling, and he found a mentor who could help him develop that skill, and to develop the part of him that was unique.

If a child is allowed to pursue what he or she believes to be his or her gift without censorship from parents or teachers, he or she learns how to ask for help, how to be self-motivated and how to be connected with their world, rather than disconnected and lost. So many young people today can only find artificial bliss in smoking dope or doing drugs, which disconnects them from life rather than engage them.

My paternal grandfather, Leo, who I always called Grand-dad, was one of the great mentors of my life. He had lived his entire life on a farm in Ronan, Montana in the Mission Mountains, surrounded by the Flathead Indian reservation. It was a special place where grizzlies, elk, deer and other wild creatures would visit his domesticated farm of dairy cows, gardens and feral cats. I spent many summers with him as a boy and cherish the memories in that incredible part of our country.

Granddad was about five-foot-six, with beautiful, gray hair, a true ruddy Irish complexion, and slight jowls that hung and wobbled when he spoke. He was the exact opposite of the stocky build of my Uncle Bill. He had steel, blue eyes and a wonderfully shaped nose that seemed to define the entirety of his face. His deeply wrinkled forehead seemed to reflect all the places he had been. He had broad shoulders that characterized his self-assuredness, and made him look taller than he really was. I loved watching him walk because he had such confidence and grace. He always seemed to be in step with the natural world and its rhythm. It gave me a sense of peace just to be in his presence, and I learned that non verbal communication could teach so much more about another person than words.

My granddad was the first person to teach me about honoring elders, not just the human kind, but the non-human kind as well. We loved to go fishing. He taught me how a fish thinks, and where they hide in order to camouflage themselves from unsuspecting insects that skip the surface of the water.

On one of our fishing expeditions I caught a huge trout. It was so much bigger than my 10-year-old mind and body was used to, that I was afraid to reel it in. Granddad grabbed the line, but he saw that the fish was barely hooked and he released it. I was pretty mad because I really wanted to eat that big guy, but Granddad explained to me that he released it because it was an elder. I had never heard anyone talk about an animal, let alone a fish, that way, but he told me that there were elders among all wild creatures and plants. The elders in every species are important, as they breed health and strength into their species. He said that that trout was needed in the trout world for his wisdom and strength.

Granddad told me that most people believed that animals and plants had no feelings or wisdom or soul. He felt that perspective was just a way to justify so much killing. The devastation that man creates can be seen all around us in small but significant ways.

When I was growing up in Santa Cruz County, there were many two hundred pound deer. Now they barely reach a hundred pounds because the hunters prized the big bucks, whose loss has diminished the species. I also remember a visit I made to the Steinhart Aquarium in Golden Gate Park, where I saw a huge, stuffed lobster hung on the wall. I heard Granddad's voice whispering in my ear, "Boy, they caught a big one, a big old elder."

Elders can be found in the plant and tree world as well. Granddad and I loved to hike and explore. He would take me to places where we could just sit with the trees. He never said that the walnut tree he loved so much was "an elder" or a tree of wisdom.   We would simply sit with our backs against the trunks and feel the variations in the bark and the hardness of the wood. We would listen to the soft music of the wind through the leaves, and marvel at the patterns the sun would create as it shined through the branches and leaves. It was a work of art, and we naturally and easily communicated that joy and pleasure to the trees.

Any time you sit by a great, old tree with an open heart you are silently communicating with that tree. The challenge for us is to receive it without questioning, to let go of preconceived notions and the fear of feeling foolish. The endless chatter in our mind drowns out what our heart so easily understands. Listening and feeling with our hearts is the key to the mystery of so many things in life, and just being in nature opens a doorway to the universe, and to a better understanding of our own internal process.

The primal urge that drives us to explore and excel in our daily lives is also the urge that drives us to explore the mystery of things. Too often I see parents who are afraid to let their children get dirty or explore the woods or even climb trees. They inhibit their child's curiosity not only within the natural world, but ultimately they inhibit their child's curiosity for life – they take away the joy of exploring the mystery and impose a false fear that is not the child's own.

With all the wonderful things that Granddad taught me, one incident has stayed with me all my life. It may not seem so dramatic, but it taught me about how to handle difficult situations. As I mentioned, the farm had many feral cats. It was an age when neutering animals was not practiced, but controlling over populating animals was necessary by whatever means.

One day I watched from a distance as Granddad gathered up a litter of kittens and put them in a gunnysack. I could see them squirming and heard them meowing and I felt frightened. I knew I couldn't speak to Granddad about it at the time, so I watched and followed him as he headed toward the river. As I approached cautiously, I watched as he threw the sack into the river to drown the kittens. I stayed hidden as he headed back to the farm.

I loved those animals and I wanted to save them, so I quickly ran down to the river and jumped in as the sack swept past. The river flowed quickly and was strong enough to drown cats and young boys, but I made it to the partly submerged sack and pulled it from the water. The kittens had been in the river at least a couple of minutes. I frantically turned the sack upside on the sandy beach and I was relieved and thrilled to find one alive; yet, I was also confused by how cruel that act had been.

Crying, and not sure what to do with the poor kitten, I headed back toward the farm hoping Granddad wouldn't be angry with me. He knew what to do alright. He had seen me jump into the river, and he was waiting as I arrived, tear-stained with a scraggly, wet kitten. He explained to me that on a farm, whether we like it or not, drowning is the form of birth control used to control the animal population.

Though I didn't agree with him, he allowed me to not agree with him without getting defensive. He took responsibility for his actions without making excuses or getting angry. He told me that sometimes in life we simply have to make hard choices. But, he also let me keep the kitten. He told me that it would always be my cat on the farm, and that I would have to accept the responsibility for its care while I was there.

Many people over the years have asked me about my leather hats. I always wear one, not just to keep the sun out of my eyes and protect my Irish skin, but I wear it out of respect for another mentor who I had met on my granddad's farm. He was a neighbor who always wore an old, leather hat. I would see him on his walks near the farm many times and every time I saw him he wore the hat.

When I was about nine years old, I actually met him as I was sitting on the bank of a nearby creek. He stopped to talk. I was still afraid of strangers, due to the hell I'd gone through with my neighbors in Santa Cruz, but my intuition told me that this man was different. I had only seen him from a distance but up close he had warm, soft eyes and a red, almost burned looking complexion. He had a gentle voice and a peacefulness about him that lent credence to what my gut was telling me.

The man said he stopped because he noticed that I was eating some plantain leaves, a wild edible that my Italian friend had taught me was good to eat. He was happy to see that I loved wild plants, and was curious about them because they were a big part of his life. He showed me how watercress grew in the creek right in front of me, and how delicious it was. He taught me about cheese-weed, and how the little "cheeses" on the leaves were edible, and how the plant's fibers could be used to make string. He even showed me how to brush my teeth with the roots of the plant, stressing how important it was to keep clean when in nature to remain healthy and strong.

Most importantly, he taught me about the sacred connection between plants and people. He told me about praying before taking a plant. As people say grace before dinner, he stressed that there is energy between plants and people, which has now been scientifically proven, and that praying and asking the plant if it would be all right to take it showed respect. Eventually I learned to feel the energy of plants, and to develop a deeper sense of communion with them as fellow living beings.

This life long skill has been the biggest factor in my success as a prolific gardener. At my outdoor school I have a vegetable and flower garden, which provides organic food for our students. My apprentices help with the gardening and at times are confused when I tell them to leave many of the "weeds". There are certain plants that don't seem like a good idea to keep in the garden or on the outskirts of the beds, but they have become friends of mine and they have their own purpose for being there, whether anyone understands what that is or not. It's just a knowing that I have and it can't, and doesn't need to be explained. It just is.

Earth Peoples believed that all forms of life, be it stones, plants or animals, are all conscious beings just like humans, and deserved the respect one would accord another human being. Plants are so vital to our existence that to acknowledge their essence seems the right thing to do. They clean the air we breathe and provide us with food, clothing, shelter, tools, beauty and companionship. Can you imagine the kind of world this would be without the diversity of the plant kingdom? Actually there wouldn't be a world.

This man also taught me how to trust people again. Our hikes in the woods and his love of nature helped to heal my young, troubled soul. One of the great mysteries of life is how we seem to get exactly what we need when we need it. I am not sure I ever knew his name, but I remember his leather hat, and the door that he opened for me into the magical world of plants. Thus, sometimes a mentor can be someone whose name you don't know or don't remember. It can be a brief but memorable encounter that can affect your life, as that man did mine. Had I not trusted my intuition I might have lost a wonderful opportunity.

It was great spending summers in Montana, but I also still loved going to Colorado to be with my Uncle Bill. Uncle Bill loved to take me riding on his four-wheeled, dirt bike over the rutted roads. He'd smoke his big ol' cigar and I would hang on to his hairy back for dear life. It was like hanging on to a grizzly bear. When he finished with his cigar he would stick the butt in his mouth, chew it up and spit it out. To this day I love the strong, earthy smell of cigars and always think of my Uncle Bill.

Our dirt bike adventures included lots of stops so we could hike into the streams to fish for trout or just explore. We found beaver ponds and he taught me how to stalk in as close as possible without the beavers becoming alarmed. Once, we found a beaver lodge that had been torn apart by a bear or a mountain lion perhaps. My uncle let me go inside to see what was left. The only entry was to swim underwater and come up inside the lodge just like the beavers. It was both exhilarating and sad. I loved pretending that I was a beaver, but I was sad that their home had been torn apart and they had been killed.

Even though the forest and all its creatures are "one", and act as one, as they are all interdependent on each other, it is still an environment of individual species. I had developed a personal relationship with nature by then and I saw those beavers as individuals – living, working and playing as much as I did. So it saddened me to think their lives could end so abruptly.

Though we tend to generalize about animals or anthropomorphize them – they are individuals, and each has a distinct personality. Spending as much time as I did in nature as a kid, I could have a different relationship with each being within the same species.

I felt honored when I could have such a relationship with a wild creature.

One of my particular passions was snakes. My uncle was constantly amused by my insatiable desire to find snakes, and when I did I would jump on them. I wasn't too smart about it when I was young because it didn't matter to me what kind of snake it might be. I'd run through the bushes, getting all scratched up just to hold one. I loved to connect with snakes – they were fascinating animals and I could hold one for hours, mesmerized by its beauty and movements. To this day, I will still dive on a snake without hesitation. Even rattlesnakes are fair game for me, although there have been a few close calls, but I love holding those wonderful buzz worms.

On our amazing forest odysseys, Uncle Bill and I encountered wolverine, marten, bears and many other creatures whose tracks could be found everywhere. He would have me on all fours in the mud studying and learning what animals had made what tracks. He would have me imagine their stories – what were these tracks saying.

Sets of tracks are like adventure books that the animal leaves behind after a night of hunting. By day you can read their tracks, picture what they did, where they've been, where they were going, and who interacted with whom. I was a pretty good tracker and fisherman at a young age and I could have trapped many animals, taking their furs as trophies, but Uncle Bill told me that over-trapping was driving a lot of these animals to extinction. He said you could hate the trappers, but they were only there because wealthy people wanted the furs.

One of my most memorable tracking experiences was with a bear. Uncle Bill and I were crazy for bears. We would seek them out, following their tracks or scat until we found them in clearings or site them on hillsides feeding on the grasses and berries.

One fall as we were fishing in a creek we found some bear tracks and followed them through a clearing and into the woods until we came upon another creek. Using our stalking skills and being as quiet as possible, and hoping we were down wind, we came upon a pool that was covered by a thin layer of ice. A bear had knocked a hole through the ice with his paw and he was pulling out a trout that had been trapped just below the surface. Watching the bear eat the fish felt like a sacred moment after following the track's story to the end. A play performed by nature for our eyes only.

Uncle Bill had many culinary lessons for me as well. He taught me to eat grubs. Like bears, we would wander the woods looking for fishing bait by pulling apart rotten logs and finding the plump, white rice-like creatures. We would take some for the bait and then he'd say, "Let's pretend we're bears." and we'd pop some of the grubs in our mouths. I began to think like a bear and see the world as a bear saw it. I'd smell things like a bear, paw the ground looking for roots like a bear, and rip a log apart like a bear. I became so bear-like that I wondered sometimes if I wasn't more bear than human.

Aside from acting like bears, Uncle Bill told me that grubs were high in protein and were a valuable food source, and something I should remember in case I ever needed it in an emergency situation. I love teaching this to my students at the school. It's like a rite of passage for each person who tries eating a grub or grasshopper or ants for the first time. It's a whole new world for them, not only to do something they never imagined they could do, but it takes them into the world of insects – another doorway into the depths of nature. Most countries outside of the U.S. do eat insects as a regular part of their rich, protein diet, but after removing ourselves from the earth's wisdom, our "civilized" country has to be reintroduced to what was once common knowledge and practice.

My uncle and I were fortunate enough to watch a great hunter on one of our walk-a bouts in the woods. We had come upon a mountain lion just as it pounced on a deer. There was a gut-wrenching struggle, a life-and-death struggle that was both powerful and horrifying to watch. The deer's death was neither quick nor painless and I was pretty overwhelmed by how long it took for the deer to die.

Though Uncle Bill tried to comfort me, he was also a realist and told me that there isn't really an explanation for why nature can be so harsh and cruel at times. Everything lives off of something. Whether we are predators or prey, we are all part of the sacred circle of life. The deer and the mountain lion were dancing the sacred dance of life and death. Uncle Bill said that nature teaches us many full circle lessons.

We left the mountain lion to his deer and we headed for the nearest creek to explore its banks. My love of creek and river exploration comes from the hours Uncle Bill and I would spend hopping from boulder to boulder, getting in the water, swimming and crawling through the mud looking more like beavers than humans.

As we splashed through the chilly waters, he told me that this particular creek would flow into a nearby river, which would flow into the mighty Colorado River, then into the Sea of Cortez in Mexico, and eventually merge with the Pacific Ocean. The clouds that form over the ocean move toward land where the moisture builds until the cloud can no longer contain the moisture. The rain falls into the canyons and creeks and begins the cycle again.

I loved my time with my Uncle Bill. Simple explanations to a young mind can have a lasting life-long effect when the mentor spends the time with his young protégé. I loved his energy and it seemed to fill me up as well. Most of what I teach today is Uncle Bill's energy coming through me.

Why I had been blessed with so many good mentors is a mystery. They seemed to appear when I needed the most help, or I was about to pass into another stage of life.

From about ages 10 to 14 a good friend of my father, Bo Almroth, made me an apprentice. Most people think an apprentice is someone who is taught a trade by a skilled craftsman. I believe an apprenticeship is where you learn not just a trade or skill, but you learn about life. Bo was an engineer by trade and a naturalist by passion. He was a six foot four inch hunk of a Swede with piercing, blue eyes, and a golden, tanned face, which told the story of his years in the outdoors.

Bo was an educated man who instilled the love of reading in me. He gave me reading assignments from J.R.R. Tolkein to Siddhartha, plus nonfiction reading assignments about historical places and events. We spent many weekends hiking the Santa Cruz Mountains along a 10-mile loop, discussing the books he had me read.

Bo taught me how to fish for crayfish in the creeks, and how to cook them with wild fennel that grew nearby. He'd take me to the beaches to collect mussels and clams, or to fish from the rocks for snapper, capazone or sea bass, all the while discussing some of the great literature. He fed my body and my mind at the same time.

He opened my eyes to art, often taking me to galleries and art shows. He spent more time with me than his own sons, as his boys weren't interested in nature, which I think was a huge disappointment for him. I was a sponge and took in everything he had to teach. He gave me so much. He literally dedicated himself to me. Part of the reason I started Headwaters Outdoor School was to find some way to repay Bo for all that he gave me. His mentoring me created the same need in me to mentor others. It's a full-circle way of living, and one in which you can get immediate benefits by giving your time and energy to a child, who in turn will pass on what he or she has learned.

Good mentors can help young people light the fires of their natural curiosity and adventurous spirits. With guidance, they can engage with life, rather than hide from it, and flow with the positive energies rather than the negative. Even a young person can mentor someone younger. There is always someone eager to learn.

In today's world, kids want to grow up too fast. I have seen seven year old girls dress like pop stars, and young boys glued to computer screens and computer games that teach nothing but violence. Overwhelmed parents too often baby sit their kids with video games and television. Some working parents can't afford after school programs so their kids are latchkey kids while they work. Kids desperately need mentors who will get them away from the computer games, which remove them from the reality of living, away from the slick, commercialized ideal of femininity, and away from the need to grow up too fast.

We assume that our kids will just figure out how the world works. There are so many kids today on anti-depressants or anger management medication because they can't figure the world out by themselves, so they disconnect and become depressed or angry. We don't come into this world with an owner's manual, but we do have elders that we can learn from. I guarantee that any parent who spends quality time with their kids, and who finds good role models for their kids will be less likely to have problem teens. Ninety nine percent of being a good parent is showing up.

I don't mean that their teens won't act out or test parental boundaries - that's part of the process of growing up and finding their individuality. It's a kid's job to push the limits and it's the adult's job to say no. When they come close to crossing the line between good or bad judgment, most of those kids will err on the side of caution due to the foundation that good parenting and good mentoring has instilled in them. They will learn from their mistakes more readily than those who have had little assistance growing up, and be less likely to repeat their mistakes.

Our kids spend most of their day in school. Our schools should be a place where they are not only educated, but are influenced positively. Our culture seems to devalue schools and teachers, yet schools and teachers have the greatest responsibility in shaping our kid's futures. I had four great teachers who shaped my perspective of the world. How many kids do you know who can say they have four great teachers who inspire them to greatness?

The first of my wonderful teachers was Mr. Robertson. He was a big, round man who must have weighed 250 pounds. He had green eyes, close-cropped hair and very powerful hands. He loved to teach science. He loved it so much that he convinced the school to let him build an outdoor lab on an acre-and-a-half of school property. He was going to teach us about the earth by creating a mini-ecosystem around a pond. This really excited me so he let me help. He gave me free reign to create, and he told me the dirtier that I got, the better. He said that if I wasn't getting dirty, I wasn't working hard enough.

This may be a shock to many, but the dirt of the earth is not dirty. Today, of course, you have to be careful of polluted areas, but plain, healthy dirt is not only beautiful, but a magnificent doorway to connect with nature. Everything we are and everything we have on this earth comes from the dirt.

I began stocking the pond by transplanting fish and frogs that I'd caught in the local creeks and lakes. I planted reeds, cattails and other native plants that I collected from various locales in my community. By the time I was ready to leave high school, I had helped turn our outdoor lab into a paradise for all the students and teachers to enjoy and to learn from, and where the teachers sometimes went to meditate and have a little quiet time. To this day, our lab is a thriving little ecosystem unto itself.

Mr. Robertson also gave me an outlet for my budding nature photography passion by using my pictures in his class lectures, which inspired me to take more and better photographs. He told me about his favorite fishing place in the High Sierra's where the fish were so numerous you could almost catch them by hand, where the mountains stretched to heaven, and the rivers and creeks ran clean. It was a place where the grass stayed green for months, and the wildlife so abundant they were everywhere you looked. He said it was a place where the gods went when they needed to connect with the earth.

Most fishermen are deaf and mute when it comes to sharing their favorite spots, but Mr. Robertson showed me on a topographic map so that I could go there myself. It was in the back-country and off trails. My father and I went there and I have been going there almost every year for the last 30 years. It has become one of my sacred places, and a place where I have taken some of my best photographs.

The other three teachers who had impact on my life were Mr. Fagrell, my crafts teacher, who strangely enough taught me how to hunt wild pigs in the Santa Cruz Mountains where he lived. The pigs wreak havoc on the meadows, and Mr. Fagrell taught me how to stalk them. He, too, encouraged my photography and would provide space at school to show them, and helped me find places in town that would show my work.

Another influential teacher was, Mr. Goody. He was my history teacher who taught me the importance of understanding the past, so that we hopefully wouldn't make the same mistakes in the future.

Last, but hardly least, was my basketball coach, Mr. Sartwell, who demanded that we give our best each time we played. As a matter of fact, one of the most spiritual moments I have ever experienced happened on the basketball court. It was a moment that you hear athletes talk about when everything comes together and the performance is flawless and perfect. I had such a moment where every pass was perfect, every fake worked, every shot I took I sunk, where my teammates and I were in perfect harmony. It only lasted a few minutes, but I felt connected to everything during that time.

I have talked about special teachers and mentors in my past, people who have guided me and invested so much of themselves in my success. My parents were also a tremendous influence on me. My mother taught me how to cook, which is a huge teaching that many people, male and female, don't get. And I can honestly say my mother loved me unconditionally. She dedicated her life to me in so many ways, which I believe helped me through the rough times.

I know that if a kid feels that he or she is loved, wanted and cared for even in the midst of the most difficult home situations, that boy or girl will usually turn out all right. It's the consistent love that overcomes the bad things that happen. I found over the years that the kids who come to me without that kind of love or consistency in their life are the ones who struggle as adults.

My father was a quiet man but he gave the same kind of energy that I received from my uncle and grandfather, but in a different way. He was an engineer who designed and built missiles and airplanes. He loved the challenge of building anything. We built a couple of kayaks that we often used on our fishing trips, and to explore the environs of a local reservoir.

One of the most important things my father instilled in me was the responsibility of being part of a household. It was my task to take care of the garden that helped provide food for our family. The garden and gardening became a life-long passion. It was a place where I could feel the spirits of the plants, and where I could immerse myself in nature, while growing beautiful vegetation to nourish my family. Gardening taught me how to get the information that I needed to grow plants in abundance and in various, challenging environments.

My father didn't spoon-feed me the information. He simply said, "You're the gardener - learn how to do it!" That taught me how to take initiative. I also had to learn about different tools so I could fix things like plumbing and wiring. One time I had asked my father how a toaster worked and the next day he presented me with a toaster that he had found at the dump, and he told me to take it apart and put it back together.

But the best gift and teaching that my father gave to me was his trust. He trusted me so much at thirteen that he allowed me to go on a summer-long rite of passage with Bo. He let me go into the woods alone as a kid even at night. As a teenager, he allowed me to fulfill a long held dream of going to Canada to live alone in the wilderness. I spent four months in the wilds of Canada exploring and learning how to live and survive in extreme situations. My father knew there was danger, but he also knew that for me to find my true self, adventure was vital for my psyche and soul. He never kept a tight reign on me because he had the wisdom to give me small responsibilities when I was young.

When he saw that I could handle those, he increased my responsibilities, each one involving a leap of faith.

Each person has the power of mentorship. Each person has
a special gift that he or she can give to another person that will
affect that person's life forever. In the giving you also receive, and
you can help the world become a better place one kid at a time.

*"Our greatest teachers are those with wisdom to listen longer
and harder to the silence. They are easily recognized by their
generosity and their grins."*

-Anonymous

"If your word is reliable and can be trusted, then your word has power and significance. When your spoken or written word is backed and validated by your physical action, then your word has credibility, your word has a reputation. This choice to speak your truth certainly will enhance your personal experience of some of life's most valuable offerings such as deeper joy, peace of mind, accomplishment, freedom, and a sense of really doing the "work" that you came here to do. Staying in tune to speaking your full truth is a full time job and practice, but an honorable, worthy one regardless of how young or old you may be. Let's do this all day, every day. After all, that's the wilderness way."

-Jim Robertson

RITES OF PASSAGE

Chapter Five

Earth people have recognized and practiced rites of passage for their young since human beings have lived collectively in tribes. It was necessary for the survival of the group to initiate their young men quickly into manhood so they could hunt and provide for the community. It was necessary to dramatically separate the boys from their mothers with ceremonies that quite literally changed the boys into men overnight. Mothers willingly gave their boys to the men, to participate in ceremonies that sometimes meant the death of one or more boys who were not ready for the challenges. Though there was the chance of literal death, the death of the boy as a child was always guaranteed.

We have no rites of passage ceremonies on a grand scale today. Although, young men often carry out their own instinctive passages by symbolically tattooing their bodies or joining gangs, we honor our young with a driver's license or the right to consume alcohol legally. Most kids today find their passage from puberty through misunderstood sexual expression or peer pressure to smoke and drink. We don't honor our youth by putting them into situations that challenge them psychologically or spiritually. Helping our boys become good citizens is really quite simple, but the path is not heeded today.

We supply our kids with technological wonders that remove them from anything resembling reality. Kids used to play outside, explore the woods, build forts, chase snakes, catch frogs, build tree houses and so much more. The natural world was as much a playmate as a best friend when I was growing up.

The greatest thing the tribes did for their young was to teach them about the connection all things have with one another. They were taught to respect the earth, as the earth took care of them and the community. They were taught to serve the community above the self, and to honor the "spirit that moves in all things" of which they were a small part.

At Headwaters, I teach a "Rites of Passage" for boys and men. It's rather strange that I need to teach something that had been so accepted and understood in indigenous cultures. It's a week long experience that helps the boys find their strengths, and push through their weaknesses in a safe environment, giving them a deeper sense of themselves and their place in the community, and ultimately the world. Ceremony is created to bridge and consciously honor the process of adolescence to adulthood.

For the men, it's a chance to reconnect with their deeper nature and to honor who they have become as men and, like the boys, to become more fully aware of their weaknesses. It helps them to push through those obstacles that keep them stuck in old behavior patterns.

I was very lucky as a boy to have Bo as my mentor. When his son, Claus, and I turned thirteen, Bo gave us the gift of a lifetime by taking us on a rite of passage with a road trip around the United States. He had us read books about other people's experiences of rites of passage. I read about the Celts and Native Americans experience of putting young men out on vision quests.

A quest was a place in the wilderness where a young man sat for days without food and sometimes without water until he had vision for his life. I read about Crazy Horse, the great Sioux leader, who went into the mountains at age fourteen, and sat for three days and three nights until his vision was revealed. I was so struck by his experience I couldn't wait to do the same. My enthusiasm didn't rub off on Claus however, and he protested about having to leave his home and friends for the summer. Bo knew the value of adventure in a young boy's life and Claus, though disgruntled, gave in to it.

We traveled in style – in a rustic, white, Ford pick-up with a roof rack, camper shell, fridge and even a toilet, bought especially for that trip. It was home to the three of us, plus Bo's dog, Julius, a German shepherd and Labrador mix. Our trip would take us to 35 states, where we would backpack and explore the wilderness and the urban jungles, from small towns to historical sites. My journey would culminate in northern California on Mt. Shasta, where I would climb to the summit, 14,000 plus feet, and spend the night alone, thinking about my future and what it is to be a man. Bo told me I would also write a Code of Honor for my life – a life map of values that I would need to keep with me for a long time to memorize so it stayed with me forever.

We loaded up the truck in early June and began our drive through the already summer-browned hills of the Bay Area. We headed northeast to Lake Tahoe and descended the spine of the Sierra Nevada range and out across the Nevada desert. Before we reached the Nevada border however, I had my first brush with death.

Bo had me make a climb that was behind some lakes near the Tioga Pass in the Sierras near Yosemite. Our base camp was at about 10,000 feet but we were still below the tree line. My goal was a steep spire much higher – up on the stark, white, granite walls – way above the tree line. I was to make the climb alone, outfit myself, find my own route and hopefully have the good sense and wits to use my wilderness skills without coming to bodily harm. I was to stay there for as long as I felt comfortable, and to do it for the love of the outdoors, and to prepare myself for the more difficult climb of Mt. Shasta later that summer.

I made my first mistake quickly by being a little too cocky and climbing higher than I should have and beyond my skill level. I became scared and lost my footing in the loose stone and half-slid, half-tumbled down thirty feet of slick, granite wall. I could see the end of the wall, and I knew I was heading for a one-way launch into the great abyss.

I had no idea how to stop myself. I was terrified, and I clawed at the granite hoping to reduce the speed of my trajectory and to stop before the "abyss". Without quite knowing how, I did come to a heart pounding stop. I had the awful taste of fear in my mouth. I lay there not daring to move for fear I would slip again. As I came to my senses and my fear became more manageable, I realized I had landed in a clearing among a herd of deer that seemed quite unperturbed by my presence. How strange that my abrupt arrival didn't even seem to register with them. I immediately felt a sense of ease and calm wash over me, and I felt pretty good among this herd. I had an eerie sense that the herd had stopped my fall. I felt as if a spirit had rushed to my rescue, for clearly if I hadn't caught hold of something permanent I would have pitched over the edge and fallen another 100 feet. I lay for an eternity feeling the mix of exhilaration, fear and relief – feeling very much alive.

As my breathing slowed to its normal rhythm and my body became centered and calm, I realized that I didn't really need to climb further as I felt that that experience was my purpose for the solo adventure. My cockiness and boldness almost took my life, while luck and spirit saved it.

When I returned to Bo we spent a long time talking about the experience, which helped me understand that luck and spirit need to be honored. To walk away from that with just a, "Wow was I lucky." would have been okay, but to see beyond it into the mystery of luck and spirit allowed me to learn about faith and trust, in a world that was beyond our rational understanding – the place where intuition comes from.

Awareness and intuition are partners. Awareness however is cultivated and learned, and intuition is felt. We develop awareness of people or our surroundings by observing what is visible. A person's body language is far more important in understanding that person than the words coming from his or her mouth. Observing clouds building on the horizon is sometimes more important than basking in the sun. Watching how people are driving before stepping into a crosswalk is more important than assuming you can cross safely on the green light. Intuition is the invisible knowing that comes from awareness. It's the thing that lets you know the person with the sweet words is angry, the clouds will be bringing a major storm, and the person driving at too great a speed is not going to be able to stop when the light turns red. So many people are oblivious to it all and wonder why their lives don't work.

My adventures with Bo helped hone both my awareness and intuitive skills, sometimes at the risk of a great deal of pain. At Cape Hatteras off the coast of North Carolina we could drive right onto the beach. There were plenty of good spots to camp and I was eager to get out of the back of the pick-up. I was tired from a long day of reading and being on the road. Thrilled that we could actually drive onto a beach and camp, I jumped out of the truck and landed squarely on top of a small cactus. I fell to the ground in excruciating pain and fear, thinking that some huge insect had attacked me. Searching the sands for some demon, I saw the cactus half-buried. Bo ran to me and was filled with almost as much horror as I, seeing my foot loaded with spines – a true pincushion.

It took Bo about two hours of pulling each thorn – they were shaped with a hook or barb on the end, which meant that Bo had to exert pressure to extract each one and I screamed bloody murder with each pull. The pain was made much greater because Claus was swimming and enjoying the water, and I was reminded of how oblivious I had been with each extraction. If it hadn't been for Julius, who never left my side during this awful process, I don't know if I would have made it. He seemed to understand and comfort me as only dogs can.

I promised myself to be extra vigilant and to pay attention to any feelings I might have. Within a day or so the bottom of my foot had healed well enough for me to swim. I loved bodysurfing and I was overjoyed to be doing it on the east coast. I felt like a world traveler being able to bodysurf in two different oceans. The joy of wave riding soon turned to apprehension when I felt my intuitive senses kick in – a dread swept over me and I stopped moving and tried to center myself.

I knew the Atlantic had lots of sharks and my heightened intuitive self was ready for anything, particularly after the cactus incident. As I scanned the horizon, I saw a group of dolphins riding the waves. I screamed for Bo and Claus to come quickly. The panic on Bo's face swiftly turned to joy at the sight, and we all swam out to meet them and to ride the waves with them. We stayed out for over an hour and as suddenly as they came, they disappeared. It was so sudden that we all wondered if it had really happened, but the moment of connection with such magnificent creatures could hardly be denied. I felt that I had been rewarded for paying attention to what I had thought would be a dreadful situation.

As a naturalist, Bo worked with a variety of plants. He taught us how to really know the plants by having us spend time with them and use our inner vision to listen to the plant. On certain hikes he would have me sit with two or three plants studying their shape and size, what grew near them, how they smelled, what kind of soil they grew in, and if not poisonous, to taste them. Did I get a feeling about a certain plant? Did an image come into my mind – which is the way a plant speaks to the people who will spend the time with it? By speaking, Bo also meant that my intuition and images gave me some visual information about that plant. This way of observing also worked with trees and rocks and grass etc.

He taught me about "owl" eyes, allowing me to see more by simply opening my eyes wider – like an owl. He taught me how to see through, around and beyond things. It's easy to see what is perceived to be in front of you, but there are the empty spaces that contain as much texture as the object. In fact, I have learned later in life through a photographer's, artist's eye, that it's that space between that allows an object to come forward, and gives it shape and definition.

Bo taught me about deer ears, using my hands as antenna and cupping the backs of my ears to move them in different directions, like the deer do to audibly pinpoint where a sound is coming from. Mimicking the auditory skills of a deer opens up a world of sound the ordinary ear misses.

Visualization is also important for developing your intuition and awareness. Bo said that visualizing something would make it so. It may not happen instantaneously, but practice and faith would open the doors to having the image materialize. Imaging is picturing events or things to come. Today athletes are taught to visualize their race to the minutest detail, as scientists have proven that visualization does work, and that it can help an athlete be a better competitor.

All these wonderful tools Bo had taught me then, are who I am today. He had the wisdom to cut me loose in a world of my choosing, and I chose to play life to the edge by experiencing the joy of nature without fear. There were three adventures that summer with Bo that allowed me to witness my adolescent life with adult eyes.

We were in the Great Smoky Mountain National Park and I had been hiking fast way ahead of Bo and Claus. I was enjoying the views and environment and thinking about what a great hiker I was. I had never seen a hardwood forest so beautiful and so different from my west coast home. All the new sights and sounds fascinated me. I was also thinking about the juicy steak I was going to have for dinner as I came around a bend and face-to-face with a black bear – we literally crashed head-on like linebackers on a scrimmage line. We were both momentarily dazed, which is probably what saved my life.

I turned and ran down the trail just as fast as I could, hoping beyond all hope that the bear was too stunned to follow. I threw off my backpack like it was on fire and continued to run for my life. I turned once or twice to see if the bear was coming, and though I didn't catch sight of it, I ran like a sprinter until I reached Bo and Claus.

By the time we got back to my backpack, I could see from the bear's tracks, the churned up leaves, squashed plants and disturbed dirt, that it had been just as terrified at bumping into me. The bear had crashed down the hill leaving my backpack untouched with my steak still inside. Even though I knew I was safer with Bo and Claus, it took my heart a long time to return to a normal beat and for the hairs on the back of my neck to relax.

We continued our hike to an Adirondack hut where we would spend the night. These huts are placed throughout the forest to accommodate about a dozen campers under one roof – it wasn't my ideal of wilderness camping, but it's where we ended up that night, and we had a fine time telling tales with the others.

As I was feasting greedily upon my steak, the hair on the back of my neck stood at attention again. I looked around the group, but no one seemed to have any concern, yet that feeling told me something was out there. I heard a noise and told everyone but no one seemed bothered. They said it was probably a deer, but I had heard deer in the woods and this didn't sound like a deer. Suddenly, as I was about to say I didn't think it was a deer, a black bear exploded from the woods into our site. He came toward us unperturbed by our shouting and pan banging. I was quite fearful after my close encounter that afternoon, and I had also just read a book about bear attacks. Even though I was afraid, I happened to notice that the bear's hind leg was nothing more than a bloody stump. The bear seemed to have no fear as he clambered into the circle and began to eat whatever food he could – my steak, someone else's oatmeal, a tuna casserole etc. When he finished he hobbled off on three legs, dripping blood from where the fourth should have been.

No one had been hurt, but the shock at such a terrible sight made all of us extremely sad. About an hour or so later some rangers came into our camp in pursuit of the poor bear and told us he had gotten his leg caught in an illegally set trap, and that he had chewed his leg off to get free. The rangers too were sad because they had to hunt the suffering animal down and kill it.

It reminded me of the writer, great tracker and tiger hunter, Jim Corbett, who said that he never found a man-eating tiger that hadn't been injured in some way, making it impossible for him to catch its usual prey; as a result, the tiger would prey upon humans. A bear with its leg chewed off would never be able to survive the rigors of the wilderness, and the easy pickings from humans meant death to the bear.

I had read about such traps in my books and some magazines, but to experience the result of such cruelty was almost too much for me to endure. The person who did that was surely as evil as the people who had harmed me in my earlier years. I loved bears. I was a kindred spirit. Big Bear was my spirit healer and guide and I felt that bear's physical pain to my core. My childhood illusions that the world is a good place were once again betrayed by adult acts of cruelty, and I struggled with not becoming bitter. Bo assured me that even though the world and life is full of pain and struggle, we must constantly choose to affirm life to right the wrongs others do, out of ignorance or fear. It's a hard lesson to learn even to this day.

Though the marauding bear instilled some fear in me, I knew that nature was still the great healer, although she did test me to my limits in the cypress swamp just south of New Orleans.

Bo encouraged me to hike alone, in part, to improve my awareness and navigational skills, but also to heighten my senses that only hiking alone can achieve. We had come to the world renowned cypress swamp in Louisiana Bayou country, and I was captivated by the huge, old trees whose trunks disappeared into the still, black swamp water. Their branches reached to the sky, dripping long strands of Spanish moss that gave them an ethereal quality. The swamp was alive with alligators, crawfish, raccoon and cottonmouth snakes, lending a dangerous, travel-at-your-own-risk quality as well. I figured what better place to hike alone, what greater adventure to have than exploring a swamp.

I ventured into its murky waters and I immediately sunk into two feet of water. The trees were a hundred or more feet tall with beautiful bromeliads growing from the trunks and branches, creating a suspended garden. The sounds of birdcalls echoed through trees, bouncing back and forth. It was an acoustically perfect, concert hall, and I was almost hypnotized by it all. My senses were so overtaken by the awe and mystery of it that I wandered aimlessly and joyfully until I realized I was lost.

I had never been lost before, and I had never been in a swamp before, so I had no idea how to get out. I couldn't use the sun as a bearing because the trees covered 90% of the sky. There was no trail, and no matter which direction I looked, it all looked the same. I felt the chill of panic and even started to cry, knowing that the venomous creatures and the alligators could make a fine meal of me.

Without my really being aware of doing it, I was hugging a tree for comfort. It seemed the tree understood my fear and I felt encouraged to climb it. It was as if the tree was telling me to climb, and to center myself, and then everything would be all right. Night was approaching and I knew I would stay put for a while. Below me alligators lurked, and the strange noises that brought such joy earlier in the day took on a frightening quality. I saw one monstrous snapping turtle - I had heard that they could be more vicious than an alligator.

As night swallowed the swamp, I wedged myself deeper into the crotch of a branch of that old tree. It was a long night of imagining all the terrible things that could happen to me. The outline of trees in the black night looked like monstrous creatures reaching out to absorb me into their netherworld. The occasional bug on my skin felt like someone trying to touch me – someone I couldn't see, and my mind raced with thoughts of swamp ghosts and spirits. But I would always go back to hugging the tree and a feeling of peace would comfort me again. It was a long, long night and I could only doze, as the unfamiliar noises always startled me awake, but once daylight crept through the Spanish moss my nighttime imaginings seemed childish. Yet, even through the fear I also felt a wonderful peace in that tree.

I scrambled down the tree and into the murky water again, not really knowing which way to turn – I tried to tune into my inner vision and voice, but the exhaustion from the sleepless night was keeping me off-center. I finally trusted the direction my intuition pointed me toward and hoped for the best.

I hadn't been walking more than ten minutes when I heard a dog barking. I was elated that there was someone else within range, and I yelled and yelled until I heard a yell in return. I ran toward the voices and was overjoyed that it was Bo, Claus and Julius. They said they had been looking for me most of the night, but that they too had quite a swamp-quest and had been turned around. Bo said that his intuition told him that I would be all right, but at that moment it didn't seem to matter, as we all hugged each other with great relief.

The night in the tree really had been a quest and a rite of passage in itself. Though I was afraid, I allowed my self to calm down and tune into my inner thoughts. It was a meditation of sorts and test, and I knew that I would find my way out if I stayed centered and in control of my fear. I felt quite grown-up after that night alone, and I grew to appreciate that the fear comes from my own mind. Certainly the snakes and alligators were real, but they were in their environment and not hunting me, and I knew I was safe in the tree. The true fear was created in my mind. I learned that if I can create it, I could just as easily replace the fear with better thoughts.

The third adventure was not really an adventure; it was a lesson in the harsh reality of life and prejudice. The Deep South in the 1960's was a place of constant racial strife and economic deprivation, that was changing with an influx of people looking for good land deals, corporations taking advantage of cheap labor and land, and retirees looking for good weather. It was a time when black Americans started to take back their lives, a time of Martin Luther King's dream, and a time when there were still "Jim Crow" laws. At that time I had never heard of such a thing.

We were driving through Mississippi when our Ford truck broke down. We found a gas station, and a mechanic, who was so covered in grease, that we figured he had to be a magician with cars and trucks.

While the truck was being fixed, we decided to have lunch, and we walked through a park on our way to a near-by restaurant. I stopped at the drinking fountain to quench my parched mouth. Before I could drink, I encountered a black person who told me that it was a "black drinking fountain" and that I couldn't drink there. I was stunned. I had never judged a person by the color of his skin. I was taught that you judge a person by what he or she does and not by how they look. I had heard about segregation, but it never entered my mind as to what it meant – that all changed in Mississippi.

The same thing happened again in the park bathroom. There were only black men in there, and one man came up to me and said, "Son, you better get out of here." I sensed his sadness in having to tell a 13-year-old, white boy to leave the black's only bathroom.

We finally found the classic American diner and I was ready to eat everything on the menu. We sat in a booth by a window and across the street on a billboard there was a picture of a hippie on it. It portrayed the classic hippie's look, with long curly hair, all kinds of beads, and a scraggly beard. Across the top and over the picture was written in huge letters "Stamp out Pollution". I asked Bo what it meant, and he said they didn't like hippies around there.

I couldn't believe that people didn't like hippies. My parents took me to San Francisco's Haight/Ashbury during the "Summer of Love" so we could be a part of history. We were sightseers and we had a great time. They seemed weird to us conservative types from Santa Cruz, but there was nothing to dislike. It was Mississippi that seemed like a foreign country to me. I had never been to a place where black people were pitted against whites, and where some whites hated black people just because they were black. It boggled my mind.

By the time we got our truck we were ready for anything. Would we be taken for a large sum of money? The mechanic charged a dollar and said it was simply a loose wire. I suppose he could have been a jerk, but he was an honest man. It was a strange day.

Our adventures took us to New York City. It was an awesome, exciting and intimidating place. I was hoping to camp in Central Park, but we found a giant parking lot that took campers instead. I went to the Empire State Building, the Statue of Liberty, whose endless stairs I climbed and, most exciting of all, the Museum of Natural History. I learned about endangered species like the passenger pigeon and the great auk, and I loved the nature displays of by-gone cultures. I could have stayed there for a week. I also loved Central Park. In the middle of a huge city is a park that's a stopover for all kinds of birds on their annual migrations. Imagine being a bird and flying over a mass of terrain that's concrete and buildings, and suddenly it changes to trees and ponds. I imagined how happy the birds must be to find such an oasis.

I enjoyed Central Park but New York and New Yorkers intimidated me. I couldn't remember seeing a happy face. I saw people living on the street and begging for food. Those that weren't homeless were rushing and pushing to get who knows where, in a short period of time. As a California boy from the suburbs it seemed so unnatural.

We knew that you couldn't go to New York and not ride a subway. As we went through the turnstile the smell of urine and the dankness of human life hit my nose like an assaulting waft of ammonia. We went down several levels of stairs to the train we needed to catch, and I was just lost in the sights, smells and the noise of the on-coming train. The doors opened and Bo and Claus jumped on, but I wasn't quick enough and the doors closed without me.

Talk about fear. There are no trees to hug for comfort in the New York City subway. I had no idea what to do – I probably should have waited for Bo and Claus to get the next train back, but I figured they would never find the right station. I didn't trust people to ask for help, so I got on the next train. I was sure people could tell that I was out of place. They seemed to be checking me out, which scared me more. I actually felt like my life was going to end because I had no idea what to do.

I decided to get off the train and find a police officer. Luckily, it was easy finding one as I had heard stories they are never around in big cities when you need one. He got me back on the right train and gave me directions that confused me even more. I tried to remember which stop, and when I did get off I was shaking, and had a heightened awareness of every sound, smell and sight. I didn't get too close to people nor did I let anyone close to me. I was like a frightened animal in the wrong territory, relying on my inner vision to get me out safe. I tried to remember which block to walk down, and which way was north and south – it seems New Yorkers rely on the east side or west side of major streets, as well as the north and south to get to their destination.

Relying on buildings and street signs was a foreign experience, but a miracle took hold and I actually made it back to the camper, and to Bo, Claus and Julius. Bo had called for help and he said that half the city knew about the lost kid, but I wondered in a city like New York if anyone really looked – there were too many strange kids walking around, and I had been one. I slept like a drunken sailor that night with Julius in my arms.

New York was terrifying, and fun, and I was glad to say goodbye. For some, New York is the ultimate experience, but there were so many things that captured my imagination that summer. In the Midwest I saw huge flocks of crows. As the day gave way to dusk, they would perch like black, Christmas ornaments in the trees along the riverbeds. The impressive song of flocking crows calling to each other against the darkening sky sent chills up my spine, and I felt a hint of sadness in my heart for what had been lost.

The crows brought to mind the extinct passenger pigeons. Millions of pigeons would darken the sky as they flew in vast flocks. People, ignorant of nature's fragility, and with thoughts of plenty, would sit on their rooftops and shoot them for sport until none were left. It seems inconceivable to me even today that millions of birds were randomly shot for sport. The last known pigeon died in 1918 at the Cincinnati Zoo. Envisioning the last mated pair of pigeons brought me to tears, but defined a life-long purpose in trying to help animals wherever I can.

I was equally moved by the battlegrounds of the Civil War at Gettysburg in Pennsylvania. The hushed, lush, green fields dazzled in the sunlight. All trace of the two-day battles that took the lives of 50,000 men have long been covered by the hand and time of nature, but the memory and the ghosts are as fresh as the daily, morning mists. A place where Americans killed Americans, where brothers killed brothers, and fathers killed sons, over a belief that it was okay to enslave other human beings. The thought and emotion of that long ago war didn't really sink in until I walked the green fields, and listened to the trees – many that had stood guard over the slaughter – whispered the horror of the past on a glorious summer day.

My world was expanding faster than my mind could comprehend all that I was experiencing. Each day was a rite of passage in one way or another. I would never again be the same person that I was when I started the trip. I was learning to be self-sufficient, and as New York taught me, how to take care and fend for myself. But Bo said that adulthood was more than being responsible. To be a fulfilled adult, you had to live a life of honor.

Today's standard barely recognizes honor. We honor corporate raiders and business people who rape the environment. We honor sports figures that make too much money, and movie stars who can barely conduct their lives off the screen. My uncle always told me that you could take everything from a man except his honor.

So what is honor? For the Irish, honor meant that giving your word was a sacred contract. Honor is speaking the truth and having integrity in one's dealing with others. When one loses respect from others their honor is lost.

Why does honor matter in a world where honesty seems like a pejorative term? If we honor ourselves, which implies self-respect, self-integrity, self-worth and self-esteem, we are able to honor others. Our lives are more fulfilling and we recognize our value in this world. It doesn't mean that life is less difficult, or there are fewer hard times, it means we have the foundation and the inner strength to overcome our trials with courage and dignity.

Someone with little honor is always looking to blame someone else in the hard times. They are victims and/or martyrs. They believe that life and the world is against them, and so it is. I had had many experiences in my early life with people who had no honor, but it didn't appear so to me until I had to really contemplate and concentrate on the meaning of honor. I remember specifically on my rites journey, on a beautiful beach in Florida, encountering a group of morons on dune buggies. This particular beach was a haven for Fiddler crabs, which I had quickly befriended. They are beautiful, little creatures not much bigger than a thumb, with one small claw and one huge claw. At certain times of the year, they come together in the millions and completely cover the beach.

I would lay on the beach and let them crawl all over me. They tickled as they crawled over my belly. I could look at them from their eye level and felt as if I was one of them. I was a mass of fiddler crabs. I spent hours by the surf looking at each one through a magnifying glass.

My bliss was rudely interrupted by the roar of dune buggy engines that sailed over the dunes and onto the beach, killing and mutilating hundreds of the creatures. Bo and I yelled at the ignorant guys, but they simply laughed at us as they continued their four-wheel slaughter. I was on my knees trying to save the ones that had been pushed into the sand, crying with anger and sadness at the same time. Bo and I stayed well into the early morning hours trying to save as many as we could, but ultimately hundreds died and became a feast for the gulls. Those were people with no honor or integrity, with no sense of the connectedness of things, and their pleasure and the pleasure of other ignorant people, will slowly destroy the beautiful places and creatures in nature.

A Code of Honor must be a heartfelt set of beliefs that has meaning for you, and you alone. Many can share the words, but the meaning of the words is different to each person. One can say I will live a life of integrity, but if you don't really understand what it is to have integrity it's a meaningless concept on a piece of paper. As the end of summer approached and we were heading back to California, Bo had me really think about what each word meant on my Code of Honor. As a pre-adult it was really hard to take in the meaning of words that would reflect the way I would live my life.

When we arrived in Mt. Shasta in late August, I saw the mountain that I was to climb, loom like a vision from another world, rising 14,162 feet into solitary space. There were still patches of snow, though most of the snow pack had melted in the heat of the summer. I was to climb that mountain and spend one night up there, in air so thin the mildest exertion can make you gasp for a breath. I was scared and I questioned my ability to climb such a peak, whose rock gardens and punishing winds, whose ice and snow and glaciers are challenges for the hardiest of souls. Bo had no doubt, and he told me that when I returned I would be a man.

He walked with me to the top of what was then the ski area at 10,000 feet, and as he turned and walked away I had a fear so great that I had to dig deep into my soul to continue alone. The climb was grueling. I had always had a great pair of legs, but a bad set of lungs due to childhood asthma. I had attacks bad enough to periodically put me in an oxygen-sleeping tent.

As the air got thinner, I sang and prayed and exhausted every religious belief I had ever learned. I would stop and sit in beautiful places, and look out over glorious vistas of green mountains. I would say, "Why don't I stay here? No one will ever know. It's as good as being on the top." But I would know, and I would have to live with a lie if I chose to say that I had made it to the top, and honesty was on my Code of Honor.

I called upon Big Bear who came floating to me from the cosmos. He gave me strength and I could visualize him pushing me up the mountain. At one point I thought he was carrying me up the mountain. I felt I was riding on his back. There were other times when I collapsed in pain. I would have to really focus on calming my breath. I couldn't let the asthma overtake me. Imagine being physically tired and trying to catch your breath through a small straw and not panic. It was like drowning or asphyxiating, yet I refused to give it power. I knew I had to pace myself and go at a speed that would allow me to get to the top.

As I slowed my pace I could take in the beauty of the mountain. I had read so many of John Muir's books about his adventures on Mt. Shasta that I pretended I was him. Even though he had almost died one winter on the mountain, he loved it with all his heart. I remembered he wrote about almost freezing to death, but even in that darkest hour he found a joy in the moment. I was determined to find the joy in each moment.

Most importantly, I kept going because I had told people I was going to do it. I was going to earn my Code of Honor, I was going to have my rite of passage, and I was going to make Bo and Claus, and even Julius proud. I was going to do it for me so that I could look in the mirror at age 21, 35, and 50, until the day I died, and know that I accomplished something really big.

When I finally did make it to the top I remember saying, "This wasn't so hard." Technically it wasn't a difficult climb, but it required a thoughtful pace to get through the tough, grueling haul. I held my Code of Honor in my hand and cried for the joy of the accomplishment, and for the inspiration I had found in each step. I memorized the code sitting on top of the peak, and it became a part of who I am. It became my heart and soul and body, not just some words on a piece of paper.

When I got to the bottom of the mountain, Bo was waiting and he knew that I had returned a man. He knew that the impact of an extraordinary quest in a sacred place can change a person forever. We hugged each other and cried full, happy tears and no words were needed to be said. The deeper mystery of the energy the mountain gave me still affects my life over forty years later, as I now live in full view of her.

My celebratory lunch was in Redding before heading down highway 5 to Santa Cruz. We were so charged by the experience of my quest that it was about an hour into the drive that we realized Julius was not among us. How could we have left him behind? With guilt and fear and every emotion you can think of, we headed back to the rest stop where he had last been let out. We called, we searched, and we hunted every place that could hide a frightened dog. We sat quietly trying to put our energy into him so he would return. We were despondent when Bo finally said we needed to move on. I couldn't let him go so I used every bit of energy I had to call Julius back. I had learned from my time in the woods that focusing all my thoughts and energy on a particular animal, could bring that animal to me. As I sat in the back of the truck using every tool I had, I thought I heard a faint bark. I yelled to Bo to slow down, and to all our amazement there he was racing toward us. It was the perfect end to a perfect summer.

I have used my Code of Honor over the years as a guide and road map for my life. Through my teenage years, my journey up the mountain stayed with me, and I would spend many hours by myself in the woods contemplating the long-term effect of that quest. I learned that my life's purpose would be to share my love of nature with people, to try and instill in them the connectedness of all things, and to respect the earth as the life-giving force that it is for all beings upon her.

As I tell many of the boys that I work with at the school, and who I put through a rite of passage, the effects of the experience might not be felt for a long time, but it will deepen and grow if they respect their code. It is my belief that when the stone of initiation is cast into the waters of the ritual, the ripples of each boy's experience will touch the life of each person he meets.

> *"Excellence is the result of caring more than others think is wise, risking more than others think is safe, dreaming more than others think is practical, and expecting more than others think is possible."*
>
> *-Thomas Edison*

"Go out in the woods, go out. If you don't go out in the woods, nothing will ever happen and your life will never begin. Go out."

-C.P. Esetes

FISHING

Chapter Six

"Think like a fish, think like a fish, think like fish" – that was my mantra as a friend and I tramped through brush toward Gray's Falls on the Trinity River in northern California, near the Hoopa Indian Reservation. It's a beautiful place where the river creates a cascading waterfall and tumbles and rumbles into the deep pools below. This is the place where the salmon congregate as they make their final push up river to spawn.

As we got closer to the sound of the river, we came upon an old-timer on his way to the fishing holes, and who incredibly, told us of all the hot spots. Most fishermen wouldn't tell a single person where their prime spots are, so we figured our encounter was heaven sent, and destined to provide us nature's bounty. He told us of one special hole that was a perilous place in the middle of the rapids, which meant we had to ford the river. He told us the earlier we got there the better, because only two or three people could fit out there at one time. He said the best way to catch them was to use a #1 hook without a barb on it. The elder suggested a bit of red cloth tied to it instead, as the salmon don't eat on this journey, because they are in such a state of frenzy making their way to the spawning grounds. They will strike out, however, at any red object that comes near them, and that's how you catch them. Sounds easy, but it isn't. With the sound of the river near us and the sound advice from the generous guy, I was pumped and anticipating some of the best fishing of my short life.

Fishing is a great tool for learning about inner awareness, and like learning about edible plants; it's a great doorway into the deeper realms of nature. Thinking like a fish should be pretty easy, since their brains are miniscule, but they are very difficult to catch, as they are instinctual thinkers. Because the fish react instinctively, they are aware of the slightest changes in light and noise.

My experience of watching the bear fish with Uncle Bill reminded me what I had to do for a successful catch. I had to be quiet, stalk and crawl to the fishing pools so the fish wouldn't see my shadow, or feel the vibration of a heavy footfall on the ground. I had to use my senses-smell, sight, hearing, touch and inner vision. I had to become one with the environment, and think like the predator who feeds upon it. I had to think like a bear, otter or heron. I would imagine myself as an osprey or a bald eagle soaring high above, so as not to cast a shadow, with eyes so alert that a flash of the fish's tail would trigger my predator instincts, as I dove silently down to catch the fish hiding in the shadows of the rocks.

As we approached the falls, the sunlight against the wet skin of the jumping fish looked like sparks of electricity dancing off the water. That quick glance sparked within me a vision of the complete lifecycle of the salmon, from the time they lay their eggs, the hatching, and the desperate swim of the newly born from the river to the ocean. I envisioned the ocean where they spend years facing the hazards of killer whales, sharks, dolphins and fishing boats, and yet, miraculously find their way back up river to the spawning grounds to ensure the survival of their species. I felt the power of the salmon journey and I felt deeply connected to the spirit of the fish.

As we made the steep climb down into the canyon, we saw a couple of fishermen claiming their rights with the flick of the rods. We also noticed some kids about our age casing the place. As the salmon frenzy began to calm, the fisherman started to leave knowing that they could dangle the red cloth all day and not a one would bite. The other kids however, had brought treble hooks that they weighted, casting over the pools as soon as the last of the fishermen had left. It was an illegal way of catching fish, as the hooks when jerked could hook the side of the fish's belly.

Large numbers of salmon can be caught this way. There is no sport or craft involved in this type of fishing - it's for the greed of the take only. We were just about to intervene when a Fish & Game warden appeared and arrested the kids, confiscating their knives and fishing equipment, and saving us from the potential bloody brawl. I hate the ruthlessness of humanity, particularly in relation to the creatures of the world who can't fight back.

I was confident from having studied the river, and how the other fishermen fished, that we could start our day early and be successful. We got up about 3:00 a.m. in the moonless night, as we wanted to be the first ones there. Though we had flashlights, they were not really helpful in the unfamiliar terrain and the opaque dark. I slipped in the darkness, and tumbled down a cliff about fifty feet, almost killing myself in the fall, but at sixteen the feeling of indestructibility is enough to heal any wounds, and I literally dusted myself off and got on with it. It was important to be there at the "magic hour" that time right before dawn, as the sky is just beginning to lighten. It's the time that the Indians and the poets say we can slip between the two worlds – the physical and the spiritual.

It sure felt sacred out there as great blue herons, river otter, eagles and all kinds of critters stirred and prepared for their daily survival. My friend and I slogged through the leg-numbing, snow-melted waters to reach the rock where we sat shivering until the first rays of the sun blessed the earth.

As the pools began to light up, we dropped our lines. Within an hour we each had caught three salmon, which was the limit. We couldn't believe our luck or how easy it had been. It was time to give the rock to others who had gotten up early, but not as early as us.

As we slogged back through the icy waters, there seemed to be an energy shift. We all sensed something. It was as if electrical impulses were charging the air and everything around us. Everyone felt it and we all started to yell excitedly to each other. "What do you see?" was the question circulating up and down our piece of river. Finally, one of the fishermen yelled, "Steelhead." I had never seen one, and in the time it took for me to say steelhead, the river was streaked with lightening bolts of silver energy. The water was pulsing and shooting up all around the salmon and us.

Like salmon, the steelhead travel from the Pacific Ocean up the rivers to spawn further in. I was paralyzed with excitement, hypnotized by the motion and the energy, as one of the old fishermen brought me back into my body by yelling to put some salmon eggs on a hook. It seemed instantaneous as my roe-baited hook hit the water and my line went screaming up river, and just as quickly came screaming back.

It was mayhem from one side of the river to the other, up and down, and I held onto my rod for dear life. The old guy yelled that I had a big one. I was putting all my energy into trying to reel it in. I was jerking the rod trying to get it in one motion, as the old guy appeared from nowhere whispering in my ear, "Softer, softer now. Not so hard, you'll lose her. You gotta work her. Let her come to you." The fish kept zigzagging and before I knew it there was a crowd around me on the banks of the river shouting encouragement and advice.

It was one of the most connected moments in nature that I had ever felt. I loved that fish for that moment. I fought it for 45 minutes, my energy waning as I pulled him closer and closer, and finally the decisive moment as someone came to my side with net in hand ready to scoop the giant into our world. He put the net to the tail first, and the fish feeling the net gave one more struggle for freedom, wiggling and lurching and jumping, loosening the hook and flying into the river and down stream. I couldn't believe it. How could the guy be so dumb – you always put the head in the net first. I was ready to explode, grief-stricken and exhausted from all the work with nothing to show for my efforts when it struck me. That fish had given me the most incredible 45 minutes of my life and he was free. He fought with everything he had and then some to get up that river to make sure his species survives. He was one of thousands, but it didn't matter to him. He was the one that would ensure the steelhead lineage.

My anger quickly became happiness. I realized that that fish's survival was more important than a good hearty meal. I never fished the same after that. I became a catch-and-release fisherman. I felt that the spirit of nature rewarded me with a sacred moment. He said, "You're doing a good job. You're one of the good ones. Keep it up. Here's a gift." His gift was the awareness of the connection we have with all things.

A year later on the same river in the same spot fishing for salmon I hooked a really big one. It made a 14-lb steelhead look puny. I fought her for about an hour and a half finally landing her on the riverbank. She must have weighed over 40 pounds and as I hauled her in and caught her eye she started laying her eggs right there on the grass. I quickly let her go hoping that there were enough eggs left in her for the next generation. I will never forget the look however. It touched me to my soul. It spoke of a lost generation, and the struggle she had had for the last seven years surviving the ocean and the sharks, and making it this far struggling to return to the place of her birth, only to be caught by a boy. I prayed that her journey would end successfully.

In addition to river fishing, there is creek fishing. You can fish the lakes and the ocean or any body of water that has fish, but my favorite is the creek. I was always on the move, exploring, looking for snakes and crayfish and harvesting wild edibles among so many other things that can capture the imagination. You can literally give yourself a pretty good meal from the fish and wild edibles, which connects you in a deeper sense to the environment.

After a day of fishing the creeks my Uncle Bill and I would spend the night in an old, log cabin that he kept up in the Rockies wilderness. It was wonderfully rustic with a big fireplace, a couple of bunks and kerosene lanterns. Once the fish were caught, eating them was just as much an art form. We would cook our catch over the open fire with a little bit of butter and some wild herbs for flavor. Even now my mouth waters thinking about those long ago fish feasts.

I miss the companionship of my uncle, and the days of pure joy alone with him in that wilderness. He showed me that eating just the filet is like eating only the cake and not the frosting. I remember his insisting that I eat the entire fish. The first time I popped an eyeball and a fish cheek into my mouth, it was blind faith that he would be right, and that I would enjoy the taste. Having that eyeball stare back at me was creepy. I wondered if the spirit of the fish still remained in that eye, and I wondered what it was thinking.

One of the creeks that I used to love to explore and fish was Stevens Creek, in what is now the Silicon Valley. It used to be a wonderful place where ferns and beautiful columbine flowers would hang off edges of rock, and clean water would riffle down through a little waterfall, making eternal ripples in the pool below. Maybe I would find a snake or a newt prowling along the clear bottom. I would hear frogs croaking, and chickadees chirping happily to insects in the sun-dappled leaves in the trees above. I could drink the water and feel its cool liquid spiraling to my stomach.

Some of my greatest memories are fishing with my dad in Stevens Creek. Being an aeronautical engineer for Lockheed kept him pretty busy when I was growing up, but he would always find the time to be with me and teach me outdoor skills.

We took the two canvas covered, wooden kayaks we built together to the Stevens Creek reservoir where we would fish. We'd gig frogs that we'd cook and eat along with our fish catch.

Even though he wasn't much of a talker, I would love spending that time with him. I liked just being with him and no words were needed. He was an honorable, truthful and caring person and I am thankful for that time.

But the lovely memories of Stevens Creek are all that's left of the place. The destruction started slowly. One day I would find some garbage somebody had tossed. Another day I would find used motor oil and a 50-gallon drum of disgusting liquid oozing into my pure creek water. Dead fish appeared everywhere after a while. Eventually all the household junk that people were too lazy to dispose of properly appeared like; washing machines, refrigerators, furniture etc. With each new pile of garbage I would cry for the slow loss of life and beauty, and finally Stevens Creek became lifeless. Today it's a culvert water cross, boxed in cement dykes filled with pollution and garbage.

Luckily, Coffee Creek in the Trinity Alps in northern California has not suffered the same fate. It's a wonderful wilderness area accessible to Bay Area adventurers. I have often fished the creek that runs into valleys, surrounded by steep cliffs and huge boulders strewn along the banks.

I loved hiking and climbing the cliffs and I always kept a stringer of fish hanging from my belt. The downside was that the stringer would invariably attract yellow jackets. I was never bothered by them as I rarely showed fear, and a few buzzing around seemed quite harmless. But they are quite the carnivores and they can eat a fish rather quickly, so I had to pay attention to protect my larder.

I always try to find the connection with a creature and this time was no different. I stumbled along the banks trying to protect my fish and trying to connect with a few yellow jackets that would have nothing of it. They were not there to commune with me on a spiritual level. They were mean and they were hungry.

In my stumbling and bumbling I stepped on a rotten log, broke it in half, and was suddenly swarmed by an entire hive of the aggressive creatures. Their biting and stinging is quite unmerciful, and they were freaking me out. My string of fish went flying as I flailed to protect my face, and other exposed body parts. I jumped into the creek hoping the immersion in water would save me from the painful bites, but those creatures are ruthless when angered and they got me even under the water. It took about 20 minutes for them to retreat. They were determined to make a feast of me. Every time I put my head under water, holding my breath for what seemed like an eternity, some of them would still be waiting when I surfaced. I finally had to swim under water and down stream to get away.

It was a humbling experience to be overthrown by such tiny creatures. They taught me that not all of nature's creatures are wonderful, particularly yellow jackets. I have actually developed quite a hatred for them and set traps whenever they show up in my camp at my school. They can be quite dangerous if a nest is around a camp or a group of them go after food. They not only sting, but they bite at the same time, and unlike bees who die after they bite, yellow jackets keep biting and stinging and they will follow their target relentlessly.

There had been a time in my life when I thought I would love everything in nature and find peace with even the most treacherous of creatures. My peace with yellow jackets comes in the form of fighting them, not so peaceful. I can rationalize fighting them, as they are willing to fight me – let the best man or insect win! They have taught me to be more aware in the woods. Yellow jackets love to make nests in the ground or in rotten logs. When you see one or two flying close to the ground you can pretty much bet that a nest is near-by. Like rattlesnakes, bears, scorpions, stinging nettles and poison oak, yellow jackets are nature's wake-up call.

The call to hunt and fish is instinctual. We didn't always go to the supermarket.

As a boy I loved the feeling of self-sufficiency every time I put a pole in the water. I pretended to be a pioneer whose family depended on the spoils of the hunt. I often fantasized about being one of the last, great mountain men. There is one particular place in the High Sierra's that takes me back to a time where I imagine the solitary, mountain man would go in the summers, just for the sheer pleasure and beauty of the spot. I often went there with my dad or friends. It was a perilous and difficult hike in those days, as the trail was not well traveled. It was made even more difficult by my asthma, which was exacerbated by the high altitude at 10,000 feet and the uphill climb. It was hard to watch my dad and friends chug up the mountain past me while I had to stop and rest and catch my breath. I learned to push through some of those limitations, but I also learned that I had limitations.

Reaching the lake was worth every breathless stop however. It was and is a breathtaking place that gives new meaning to "God's country". Twenty years ago the fish were so plentiful you could almost talk them into your net. One day I literally caught 60 fish – catch and release of course. I would like to say it was sheer genius and intuition, but it was really the ants that showed me.

As I was trying to figure out the best spot, I let my awareness be my guide. I observed a spot where fish were coming into the shallows and wiggling up to the edge of the shore to suck in ants that cruised by. I had never seen such a sight, and since I couldn't put ants on my hook I figured that the fish probably would eat any of the local critters, so I went on the hunt for the best hook critter I could find. Fortunately for me, and unfortunately for them, it was grasshoppers and the observation of ants that gave me one of best fishing experiences of my life.

Not everyone was in bliss though. Unfortunately, one of my friends had suffered for a week without going to the bathroom. He had never camped before, and as a creature of habit he could only go on a toilet. Had I been more aware of his discomfort I could have given him an earlier lesson in how to go in the woods. I assumed people knew how to do something so natural, but I guess we're so far removed from nature that many people need a lesson in the basics.

A chapter on fishing isn't complete unless you have a story about the "huge" fish that got away. With my new driver's license in hand, my fishing buddies and I were headed into the Central

Valley in a Corvair convertible with our poles, our shotguns, and bows and arrows. We were a sight I'm sure. The plan was to hunt for doves and rabbits with the guns, take carp with our bows and arrows, and fish for catfish at night.

The Central Valley was filled with grazing cows and bulls in our dove hunting grounds, so we had to be extra careful around the cattle, not because we could miss and shoot them, but because the bulls would charge us. I had one bull chase me for what seemed like a mile before I could jump a fence to safety. Doves are hard to hunt because they fly very fast and they swerve, so we had to focus on them while trying to focus on not being charged. It was pure adrenaline fun.

The second day, we fished for carp with our bows and arrows. They like to swim in the shallows among the tulle reeds, so bows and arrows are the best. It always reminded me of pictures that I saw of how the Indians had hunted a hundred years ago. Most people think carp aren't very good, but roasted slowly over a fire they're as gourmet as a meal can get.

The most fun I had on that trip was sitting on the bridge at night fishing for catfish and talking to my buddies. We'd lean our poles on the side of the bridge railing with our lines dropped into the water. The lines had little bells on them that would ring if a fish nibbled, so all we had to do was wait for the bell to ring while we partied away.

We'd been catching fish off and on for most of the night when my bell started to ring, but it didn't seem like an ordinary jingle. I had the feeling that this was one big fish. I was far enough away that I had to scramble and run to reach the pole. I was running as fast as I could when the rod yanked flush with the railing, and then flipped up through the air and down into the river. I shined my flashlight into the river hoping some miracle would give it back to me, only to watch my reel being hauled away at what seemed like 90 miles an hour. I knew that was a big fish, I knew that was the kind of fish books are written about – but it got away. Not only did this monstrous fish that would have made me famous get away, but it also got my rod and reel, which was some of the finest equipment money could buy, and I had worked long hours to buy them. My one hope had been that the poor fish was able to shed the hook and get free of the rod and reel.

Hunting and fishing with friends is a bonding experience that also speaks to the primal parts of our soul. Like any venture, we need to be vigilant so that we don't take it to extremes. I can certainly understand how easy it is to kill more than one needs. There is a killing frenzy mentality that can overtake you once you're focused on the hunt. To really connect with nature we need to understand that killing is also a part of nature's rhythm. It is how humans have survived for centuries before supermarkets. It's the way people lived in nature, how they participated in the cycles of life and death. Taking life is a great responsibility. Responsible hunters and fishermen today respect the process. They take only what they can eat, which honors the life of the animal they have killed.

We need to be humble again. We need to come back to the center within ourselves and the center within our community. Our extremes have created chaos and alienation. It is said that there are two ways that people make change in their lives. The first is because they want to, and the second is usually due to an illness or if something hurts bad enough. I think the same options apply in regard to people's attitude toward nature. Small groups of concerned people will always act locally and globally, but it will take the loss of a healthy planet before many people will act.

"Things which matter most must never be at the mercy of things which matter least."

-Goethe

"Walk away quietly in any direction and taste the freedom of the mountaineer. Climb the mountains and get their good tidings. Nature's peace will flow into you as sunshine flows into trees. The winds will blow their own freshness into you, and the storms their energy, while cares will drop off like autumn leaves."

-John Muir

HUNTING

Chapter Seven

Dawn was a few hours off. The marsh smelled of waterfowl and the occasional squawk or quack filled the blackness as I tried to quietly crawl through the tulles. My 12-gauge shotgun seemed a bit heavy for my 10-year-old arms, but I was determined to find a place to sit quietly and wait for the first light. I wanted to get to my spot a couple of hours before the dawn. I knew that slogging through the wet marsh and tulles would create a disturbance, and the concentric rings of that disturbance would need to settle before I could become invisible to the birds.

This was my first duck hunting experience with my dad in the Merced National Wildlife Refuge. It was full of birds, countless ducks and geese and other migratory birds that come to these marshlands for rest before their journeys' north or south, depending on the time of year. I was ready. I was excited and going over all the rules that I had been taught about getting birds. I had to aim a bit ahead of the bird as it flew so I wouldn't miss when I made the shot. We didn't have a dog so I had to shoot over open water so I could see where they landed when they fell. If they fell into the tulles they would be lost.

As the sky lightened, the sound of waking birds was deafening. One by one they would start to fly. I had my eye and my aim on a mallard as it flew over. It was a beautiful bird, flying low and fast in the dawn light, its wings whistling in the cool morning air. I led the bird and fired. Boom! It was like the bird had hit a brick wall. It tumbled and spiraled and hit the water but it wasn't dead. It was flapping and spinning and squawking – wounded, but not dead. My father matter-of-factly told me that I had to go out there and break its neck. The thought was gruesome, and each step into the marsh was painful, as I knew that I would have to have the courage to break its neck when I reached it.

As I approached, it stopped flailing and I prayed that it had died, but such moments are rarely that easy, and I found it to be exhausted and wounded. The bird's eyes connected with mine in a "forever" moment, and as I picked up the poor creature from the water, I apologized. "Sorry my friend, I have to kill you. I didn't do the job right to begin with. Please forgive me." I held the bird to my chest and wrung its neck, then stood there in tears holding it in my hand.

My father shouted, "Get back in here! There's more hunting to do." He knew however, and understood the sacred responsibility that comes with hunting. He knew how difficult it was to experience killing an animal for the first time, but he also knew hunting is taking life, and life feeds upon life. Yet, knowing that each animal has its own unique place on this earth just like us, it's still hard to kill a being that has a right to life.

A good hunter respects the bond between hunter and prey. In primitive times, indigenous people would pray before and after a kill to announce their good intentions and to give thanks to the animal spirit. The hunters considered that the spirit of the killed animal entered their being when they ate it, and that they had a responsibility to honor the soul of that animal. They believed that the animal spirit would be present the next time they went on a hunt and assist them so that others of its kind would give up their lives when needed.

I remembered these stories and I gave thanks to that duck for giving its life to me. I knew that that duck and the others that I killed that day would provide food for my family for quite some time. When I killed, I would often sit quietly with the animal, admiring its form, thankful and reverent for what it was about to give me. The animal would often come to mind for days after I had taken its life, its spirit reminding me of the gift it gave.

I didn't always hunt with a shotgun. I actually found hunting with a self-made tool much more rewarding. I searched for two weeks looking for the perfect Y-shaped stick so that I could make a slingshot. I fastened an old piece of rubber from a tire's inner tube to the prongs, and I had one wonderful slingshot. I practiced shooting small stones at river rocks along a creek and I became a pretty good shot, at least at stationary targets.

One of my first kills with the slingshot was a typical young boy, thoughtless act. I saw a robin from my bedroom window perched on the telephone wire in the front yard. I aimed not really thinking I would hit it. Not only did I hit it, I demolished it with the velocity of the careening rock.

I loved robins. They were always the first bird to sing praise to a new day in the morning and give thanks for the day at dusk. I loved their color. I loved watching them peck worms out of our lawn. I actually helped them after rain storms by picking worms out of our gutter and putting them on our grass like bird seed. So when I found the bird dead from a big hole in its chest due to my rock I felt horrible, and I vowed not only would I never kill another robin, but I would also protect all song birds for the rest of my life. It took some regretful experiences to gain the understanding from my own thoughtless, impulsive actions. I learned how one can make bad choices that result in consequences you can't take back.

Even today, as a result of that negative experience, I have continued to turn it around into a positive, and I have created a sanctuary on my land where hundreds of migrating song birds come to eat, drink and rest. I have dozens of nesting boxes and a sacred space for them where even my dogs are not allowed to go so they won't be disturbed.

After having killed that robin I knew that I had to eat what I killed out of respect for the creature. To randomly kill animals for no other purpose than to kill is a wanton cruelty and disrespect for all life. So the next day I made a small campfire in the woods and I roasted that tiny creature along with some squirrels that I had shot, and consciously ate them with reverence.

Many Native American tribes would construct buffalo shields in honor of the buffalo that they killed. The best tribal artists would decorate the shields, which they would eventually burn in ceremony, honoring the creature that gave them life.

The robin gave me my first "medicine" feathers and her wings were dried and used as power objects. Meaning, I was then aware of using the qualities of the robin in times of need. I called on the tenacity, endurance and joy of that bird many times.

In addition to slingshot hunting, I learned how to set dead-fall traps and snares for rabbits. One of my traps had snared a rabbit and I found it hanging upside down and still alive. I approached quietly, but the rabbit was terrified and started screaming. The sound was so human-like and penetrating that I literally began to spin from confusion and fright. I had to sit by a tree and calm myself before I could go back and cut the rabbit down. Luckily for the rabbit and for me, he had not been injured. The snare had caught him around a leg and the chest so he was just scared. I held him for a minute while I apologized and petted him and then let him go. I suppose I could have killed him, but his fear was so palpable that I could only feel compassion, and felt that it wasn't his time to go. It was meant to be a teaching experience for me.

I think a good hunter knows when to keep an animal and when to let one go. It's a visceral, heart connection that you can have with an animal, rather than a kill for pleasure and power thing, which unfortunately can motivate so many hunters. Being aware of that connection possibility is really important when you are in the woods. Listening to your inner vision, your intuition leads to a greater connection with the natural world. Part of that asking though is that you have to be willing to hear, "No." and respect that voice without maybe a clear understanding as to why in that moment. We tend to take what we want when we want it, rather than allowing room for another option to present itself.

I had many hunting experiences as a kid, but truth be told they have always been difficult. I suppose it's because I wasn't really hunting for survival, but for experience. One of my first hunting experiences was in the Trinity Alps with a family friend, Bob Smith. He was a handsome man, muscular, six-foot-four and square-faced with thick eyebrows and sharp green eyes. The thing I remember most was that he wore the same outfit every time I saw him – blue jeans, a blue jean shirt, chunky, black work boots and a really big watch that had all kinds of gadgets on it.

Bob took me to an area in the Trinities where very few people went. We backpacked in the wilderness about five miles and scouted the area for three days without our rifles. The time spent scouting was to connect to the land, read the animal tracks and keep our eyes peeled for any good size bucks. Bob said that we weren't here to take the largest animal. The biggest bucks were the strongest and were needed to help keep the deer populations strong during the breeding time.

Because hunters use their rifles to take the "trophy" animal, the deer populations breed smaller individual deer because the large bucks aren't able to pass on their genes to a significant number of fawns. The best hunters don't try to alter the balance in nature by bagging the trophy animal.

It was better to follow the example of the deer's natural predators such as the mountain lion. The lion is more likely to take something smaller because the big bucks are harder to kill, and it poses too great a risk of injury to the mountain lion.

The abundance of wildlife in that spot in the Trinities was almost overwhelming. I saw bears and wolverine, marten and fishers. The deer tracks were like a road map to where the best hunting spots could be found. We started early in the morning and walked quietly along a deer trail. We decided to part ways so that Bob was on one side of the valley and I was on the other. The idea was to flush the deer down to the end of the valley into a box canyon that we had discovered the day before.

I soon heard the sound of a deer footfall snapping the dry twigs in the distance. I stopped and sat motionless hoping he was coming my way. A young buck came into view perhaps fifty yards away, stepping warily, ears alert, sniffing the air. It was not stopping to feed even though there was a bounty of lush plants at its feet. It sensed my presence, but it couldn't smell or see me. I took aim. I had the deer in my sights and I felt from deep inside that it was right to pull the trigger. I made a good shot.

The deer was dying, blood was coming from his mouth, and his eyes were wide open when I approached. I held him around the neck and cried. Even though my intuition said that it was my deer to take, my heart was heavy from the killing.

Bob came running and he was very supportive, as he knew the thrill and the pain of one's first deer kill. We dressed the deer and cleaned him up and took him back to our camp, ecstatic that we would be eating deer steaks over an open campfire that night. It was some of the best eating I had ever had.

I used all the deer. I took the hide home and made it into rawhide for lashing my shelters. I also used a large piece to stretch over a wood rim to make a drum. The deer legs also made wonderful handles for rattles. Being able to use the whole deer made me feel like the hunter of old, who didn't waste one bit of his kill and honored its life completely.

As good as our meal was it was my game and Bob was feeling a bit out of sorts because he hadn't gotten a deer. For two days we scoured the mountains, and though Bob was an excellent hunter, the deer eluded us. They managed to stay just far enough out of the away for a clean shot. I remember on the third day we were up on a promontory taking in the incredible view and look-ing for deer. Without warning, a crack sounded loudly behind us and a bullet flew through the bushes right by our heads.

Bob looked at me and said, "That's it, I give up deer hunt-ing."

And to my knowledge he never hunted deer again.

Some of the other hunters wanted our spot on the promon-tory and they were sending a deadly message. We had no idea where the shot had come from, but we knew it wasn't far off because the loud pop and the bullet reached us at about the same time.

I tell you to this day I believe that it was a message from spirit and nature saying it's time to go home gentlemen. We had spent two days without being able to get close to any more deer. Nature was inviting us to leave and when we didn't get that mes-sage, it sent a message in the guise of a wacko hunter with a 30.06 to let the bullet fly by our heads.

I had such a good time with Bob and the experience had been wonderful. I went a couple of other times hunting small game with Bob and his son Ben. Ben was wiry with long, curly blond hair and he had his father's eyes. He was a pretty good boxer and we often sparred together. Even though I was bigger and more confident, he always managed to get a punch in that would waste me. We were pretty good friends, as he loved hunt-ing and fishing and traveling as much as I did.

My last trip with them became an out of character and unex-pected event however. The three of us went on a hunting trip to the Central Valley. They told me we would be hunting rabbits, but we never got out of the pick-up as we usually did to scour the environment. I had a bad feeling. I wanted to be part of the group, a good sport, so I didn't say anything about feeling uncomfortable at that point. But the bad feeling became an ille-gal, sickening reality when Bob and Ben took turns shooting rab-bits from the back of the pick-up as the other drove. They shot what seemed like hundreds of rabbits. They wasted them and left them behind.

Once, they stopped to toss an M-80 into a rabbit hole, laughing hysterically at the thought of rabbits being blown apart. When they came across a pool of water with catfish in it they threw another M-80 into that – and laughed hysterically again as the fish floated to the surface.

I was quite literally in shock. I was sick to my stomach. I tried to say something about them randomly killing animals and leaving them where they died, but they kept ignoring me. They didn't even ask why I wasn't shooting. It was like they were possessed by an evil spirit, and I wasn't strong enough in my power to demand the carnage to stop. It's hard at any age to have the ability to say "no" or "stop". It's difficult to not let the group mentality overtake you. I had been pretty good at it even at a young age, but I hadn't been good enough on this trip until their final act of cruelty.

At one point we were actually walking along a dirt road rather than staying to the tailgate of the pick-up. We happened to flush a coyote out of the bushes and it took off running, but not fast enough for Ben or Bob's shotguns. They were pumping as much shot into the air as the reflex action of their trigger fingers would allow. Inevitably, a bullet hit the coyote's hind leg. Well that did it for me. I started screaming in a fit of rage. I tore into Ben with my fists. I beat him and beat him, almost knocking him out until Bob walloped me from behind and knocked me off of Ben.

I don't know what happened to that coyote. I prayed that his wounds were not serious enough to curtail his hunting and eventual death from starvation. Needless to say the drive home was tense and that was the end of our friendship. I could never be around them again after witnessing such callousness towards animals, and I am sure that I would have been a reminder of their dishonor.

My old friend, Charlie Storm Owl, gave me a Cherokee teaching when he told me that a person is like a tree with two big forks growing from the trunk. The forks represent our dark side and our light side. If you lean too far to one side, your branch peels right off the tree and you're no longer whole. Same thing happens to people if they ignore or favor their dark or light side over the other. We become unbalanced. Life's great journey is finding the right balance between our dark and light natures. It's the wise person who can see that one side is dominating at any one moment, and to bring himself or herself back to center.

Personally, I believe that anyone who shoots rabbits from the back of a truck, blows up fish and blasts coyotes for fun, is not only a poor sportsman, but a person with no self-respect. And yet, Bob had been so good with me on my first deer hunt, and his son had been a great friend. It was baffling to me that the people that I had come to like and hang out with had such a dark side.

They certainly didn't have nor understand the concept of self-mastery. Self-mastery comes from a place of power within us. We engage the world by being present, and from a place of self-knowledge, experience and wisdom. The lack of self-knowledge and mastery casts us adrift with no plans or guiding principles. We flutter from one experience to another, never understanding the consequences of our actions, or how our actions and our response to external forces come from within us. We are not victims to the vagaries of life, but the creators of our life.

When we create a world that is disrespectful to other human beings and other living creatures, we create our own hell. A person like Bob fails to see that animals are individual, living beings that deserve to live on this planet as much as we do. The earth is a powerful living force unto itself. It sustains all life and the earth needs us as much as we need the earth.

"If you talk to the animals they will talk with you and you will know each other. If you do not talk to them you will not know them and what you do not know, you will fear. What one fears one destroys."

-Chief Dan George

"In all our deliberations we must be mindful of the impact of our decisions on the well-being of the seven generations to follow ours."

-from the Great Law of the Iroquois Six Nations

PLANTS AND GARDENING

Chapter Eight

George Washington Carver was a renowned plant chemist, and one of the great geniuses of American history. He invented crop rotation, and developed innovative uses for many agricultural crops from peanuts to sweet potatoes. He was once asked how he came up with his ideas. He said that he would get up at 4:30 in the morning and take a walk alone in the woods where the spirits of the plants would talk to him, and give him information on what to create. "Anything will give up its secrets if you love it enough." he said. "Not only have I found that when I talk to the little flower or to the little peanut, but I have found that when I silently commune with people, they all give up their secrets if you love them enough."

Plants taught me to see the world more deeply and intricately. I learned to pay attention to the subtle differences in the shapes of leaves, and became aware of the infinite variety of colors, including the countless shades of brown. Plants provide a doorway into the deep mysteries of nature and life. They can grow in the most difficult places, like the cracks of sidewalks or in a back lot landscape of filth. A plant's tenacity toward life is really remarkable. Think of burned out landscapes where everything seems to be destroyed, and within a month that landscape will be sprouting new, green growth.

When I knew I wanted to live off the land I learned to identify as many plants as I could. I had to learn to use different eyes to see the plants for their various uses. I needed to be able to use hardware eyes to know which plants or trees would make good shelters, fire, cordage and tools. I needed to use my grocery store eyes to find food and medicines. I knew that there would be times when plants would be all there was to sustain me. And although it was important to stay alert to the plant's uses, it was also important to just see the plants with an artist's eye and appreciate their beauty and smells.

One of my favorite things to do on my adventures was to walk along the redwood-shaded creeks observing the plants. I would create a menu with what was available as I walked. I knew that watercress loved the moistness of creeks, and could provide a pretty good soup when steeped in water with a little chicken bouillon added. There were so many plants dancing merrily on the banks that provided nutrition in addition to beauty, that I never felt scarcity in my wandering.

I do my best to use my intuition and compassion when gathering plants and caretaking the woods, just as I do when hunting or fishing. As a caretaker of the land here at my home it is necessary to take some of the trees down for fire safety and for the over all health of the woods, but as with any community I am always aware of leaving the elders. A forest without elders is a very empty forest. It is like a child without parents left there to fend for himself.

If you are truly in tune with your environment you can sense which plants are ready to be harvested, or which trees are willing to be cut for bow making. When you pull one plant from the ground rather than another, pay attention as to why you did that. Was it your intuition, your inner vision, telling you that the plant you chose also chose you?

My mother loved houseplants, so we had lots of plants bringing life to the inside of our house. All the houseplants had a life force and power, but my favorite of all plants as a kid was really a giant, apricot tree that grew in our backyard. Because it was the only orchard tree in our yard, its branches could spread out unencumbered by other trees. As a result, it produced enough apricots to feed our family and all our friends, plus the countless animals who loved the bounty when it fell to the ground. I could sit in that tree for hours eating the apricots. I have never found another tree quite like that one that produced such sweet tasting fruit. Even today, I can barely eat apricots, as they don't even come close to that succulent taste I had as a kid.

Because of my love for that tree, my parents gave me a small plot of land in our yard and told me I could create a garden. It was going to be a functional garden, as well as a garden of great beauty.

The first thing I did was to dig a hole for a pond that I lined with cement to keep the water in, rather than seeping into the ground. I collected wild grasses, tulles, cattails, mosses and other water plants, which I planted around my pond. I scavenged some pine trees that had been tossed out in a lot behind a local, grocery store. I brought in frogs, snakes and fish that I'd caught, and soon the pond became my Garden of Eden. I had made a promise to myself to use only plants that I had gathered from nature, and not one single store bought plant was used.

I expanded beyond the pond and created a fruit and vegetable garden that provided most of the produce for my family. It was such a joy and feeling of self-reliance to be able to provide a couple of year's worth of food for our meals.

The gardens became a great teacher for me, as I could experience first hand the connection between nature and plants and man. I learned what it meant to be a steward of the land as well. As I did my caretaking of the gardens for my family, I also provided a haven for insects, raccoons, skunks and countless varieties of birds. I noticed that when I quieted my mind and moved at nature's rhythm, that I could hear the language of the plants.

They spoke in their own unique way and I could see spirits or beings that lived around the plants.

These mysterious beings of light created halos around the plants, which I call earth spirits. I have also heard them called divas. They always seemed to be around as flickers of light or shapes, and colors or quick movements. I was amazed by these life forces around the plants, and I knew by working with them and with the animals, that I could create a partnership that would make my garden grow with great bounty.

I also loved sticking my hands in the dirt, knowing that it too was full of life, and getting a reminder that life exists below the surface of things. The more I learned about gardening, the more I learned that there were most likely more living things in the dirt than above it. It almost became too painful to dig so much life up, but the synergy between what's above and below was demonstrated every day in the growth of my garden.

The garden kept me nature-centered and inspired. I had incredible food, beautiful pine trees and an amazing pond that I would get into on occasion. Feeling the lusciousness of the wet and mud helped to remind me of the good things in life, while all around me the woods were being chopped down, the mountains were being trucked away for sand, and the orchards were being wiped out for housing tracts. I can't imagine how I would have sustained my sanity watching the destruction of my childhood paradises unless I had that garden.

Being surrounded by the beauty of plants always made me smile. I remember as a child one of my greatest joys would be to lie in a sunny meadow and roll in the tall grass among the flowers. I once heard it said that flowers were how the earth laughed. I'd have to agree.

Gardening speaks to the creative gift that humans have. We have the ability to adapt to different environments, which can cause destruction, but we also have the incredible ability to co-create sacred spaces. We have the potential to not only care take, but to enhance our environment as a whole by listening to its needs and desires.

Imagine every day an Earth Day. Imagine every day is a day to celebrate the earth; when each day begins with a conscious awareness of your home. Just as you celebrate your car and your clothes, and your electronics, imagine you take the same celebratory joy in your earthly home.

Imagine a day when you are stressed or depressed and you get into your beautiful car and drive to a place outside the city where you can hike a short distance and sit beneath an equally, if not more, beautiful oak, redwood or maple tree and listen to the caws of ravens or the screech of hawks. Imagine such a place where you can find comfort, solace and quiet from a harried day, a place where you can connect with yourself again; a place where you find the replenishment you need to return to the space of your cherished things, with gratitude for all that life has given you.

You can be an earth steward even in a concrete jungle and create this space in your own home environment. You can plant flowers around a tree growing from a planter in the concrete sidewalk. You can grow your own potted garden on a balcony or windowsill, and looking up in the sky on a clear, full-moon night, and fully taking in the beauty and awe of that moment, even as car horns honk, you can connect to the mystery felt by your ancestors.

Whether you love the earth quietly or loudly, love it wholeheartedly.

> *"You make your living by what you get. You make your life by what you give."*
>
> *-Winston Churchill*

"Experience is not what happens to you. It is what you do with what happens to you."

-Anonymous

SNAKES, LIZARDS, INSECTS, BATS – OH, MY!

Chapter Nine

Snakes, lizards, insects and bats are misunderstood creatures. Having a phobia for these creatures is a learned, false fear, and one generally picked up at a very young age by assimilating an adult's reaction. Certainly some of these creatures are poisonous so you don't want to go grabbing them like a cute puppy, but you can learn to respect these beings that are vital to the earth's balance, without becoming unglued upon seeing one.

I love all creatures, poisonous or not. I remember freaking out my Uncle Bill one spring while we were walking in the foothills of the Colorado Rockies tracking a mountain lion.

I was about 11 years old, and he was teaching me to pay attention to the soft ground and the disturbed leaves to see if they might hide an animal track in plain sight. It had rained for a couple of days so the wet earth created a soft outline of lion tracks, but it still took some focus and getting on my knees to really see if the ground was disturbed by a mountain lion or not. I figured that actually seeing one of the great cats was a long shot, but I loved walking in its tracks, trying to feel its energy and knowing that it had just walked that way a short time before. I wondered if it knew that we were on its trail, and if perhaps she or he was watching us from a cliff or tree above.

We never did find the lion, but at one point along the trail I heard a disturbance in the brush. Without thinking, I dove into the tall grass hoping to catch whatever might be lurking there. I grabbed a handful of earth and something else to my uncle's horror as he screamed, "It's a rattlesnake." When I realized what I had caught I quickly slid my hand up around its head and held it tight.

I didn't know before I jumped that it was a rattlesnake, but it didn't freak me out once I had caught it either. I sat quietly with it for a time, lightly stroking the snake's body and it seemed to calm down a bit. I let go of the head when it seemed pretty docile, and it actually crawled around my leg and slithered on down the trail. Even today whenever I see a snake I have to catch it and hold it. I just love connecting with snake energy. Snakes really understand human fear. I think they can pick up the scent of fear through the incredible sensors on their tongues. If you don't show fear, but remain calm and open up your heart, they will generally relax and be with you.

As a kid on my many hiking adventures, I would often encounter rattlesnakes on the trails that were curled up, rattling and ready to strike, but I would stop, remain calm and stay out of striking distance. I noticed that most of the time the snakes would calm down pretty quickly and stop rattling. Interestingly, if I even thought about killing it or acted angry or upset, the snake would immediately raise its head, shake its rattle and prepare to strike.

In general I loved all snakes, but my favorite of all was and still is the bull snake. Growing up I had over 30 snakes, a dozen lizards, 20 or so frogs and countless other amphibians and insects in my room, in different aquariums and terrariums that I bought and made. After a while I would let some go and bring in other critters. I have to hand it to my parents who never complained – their only request was to keep the door shut.

One day I came home from school and noticed that my big gopher snake was gone. I didn't want to tell my parents for obvious reasons, and looked everywhere for it without trying to arouse suspicion. I figured if I couldn't find it, it had gotten out of the house.

A couple of days later, I heard my dad shouting my name. He kept screaming for me until I came running into his bedroom where he was pointing at the closet, and telling me quite excitedly that there was a rattling noise coming from the darkness within. He asked if I had caught another rattlesnake and had let it go in the house. I assured him that I would never do such a thing, while I moved some boxes aside to find my poor gopher snake rattling away like a rattlesnake. It's one of their defenses and a good one at that!

Many animals take on a disguise sound – the jays often make noises like a hawk - to warn off predators. It taught me a pretty good lesson as well – never to take these creatures for granted. I wondered if it hadn't found a closet that was used frequently, if it could have starved to death somewhere. As a result of that awareness of their vulnerability, I would often stop when I was on my bike to move a snake or a frog from harm's way. I even made my father pull the car off the side of the road on a couple of occasions to get an animal off the road. I found that just doing that simple act connected me even deeper with nature.

Another misunderstood creature is the bat. We have demonized these poor creatures in literature so that people think of vampires when they see a bat. When I was about 11 years old, my friend, Jay Kearny and I loved to hang around an abandoned house at the end of my street. We were sure the house was haunted because we had read a few Hardy Boys books and seen some scary movies that closely resembled the old house down the street. It had broken windows and a yard full of weeds so high you couldn't see the front windows. It was dilapidated with rotten, wooden boards falling from the walls and ceilings, and it smelled musty like we thought a real haunted house would smell. We decided to explore the place one night so we could see the ghost or ghosts who inhabited the place. We were afraid that the owner might show up unexpectedly that very night, but the thrill of adventure was more than the fear of getting caught trespassing. We decided to go just before night fell so no one would see our flashlights.

It was a big three-story house, and I figured that I would work my way up rather than down, so I climbed the stairs all the way to the third floor. I had a flashlight that I used only when I couldn't see any definition. The third floor was dark with just a hint of dusk creeping through the holes so I flashed the light on and found a hatch in the ceiling. I slowly opened it, pulled down some creaky, folding stairs, and climbed into the dark attic with the light off. By the time I reached the attic floor I was covered in cobwebs, and I decided to turn the light on again to make sure I wasn't covered with any black widow spiders. As soon as I turned it on, I was surrounded by a rush of wind, created by flapping bat wings as they let go of their roost. I was so scared that I almost fell back down the hatch.

When I realized the bats weren't attacking me, and that my light had scared them, I immediately turned it off and listened as they began to settle back onto their roost. I knew as it got darker they would start to leave for their nightly hunts, but for that brief period they actually calmed me by their flying and roosting, and I stayed for a while just communing with them in the waning light.

The next day I went back at dusk and waited outside the house until the bats – hundreds of them – flew into the night to feed on the countless insects and pollen. I also sneaked back into the house a number of times to sit in the attic with the bats. Though there were a couple of inches thick of bat guano, and it smelled quite nasty, they somehow kept pulling me in. They were a mystery and I liked being with them.

I was troubled even at that young age by the reaction people had to bats. When I tried to tell people about them and my experience, they would get grossed out and tell me that I'd get rabies or other diseases if they bit me. They told me just breathing in the bat guano could kill me. We humans are a peculiar lot who try to poison poor, little mammals that actually make our lives better by catching insects. If we didn't cut down so many trees, even the dead ones where bats like to live, we wouldn't have so many living in our attics.

Another critter that most people are afraid of is the spider. I read once that if all the spiders on earth were gone, life would end in seven days because all the insects would defoliate all the plants. Spiders eat so many insects that they keep the insects in check.

When I was six years old I had quite an encounter with a spider. We were living in San Diego on a farm, and my young mind and hands were into everything. I had put my hand into a woodpile and felt a pretty good bite. I yelled for my parents to come see what had bitten me, and as we pulled away the wood my father found a black widow spider. It caused me severe pain and I remember having to go to the hospital. I don't quite remember what they did for me, but I do remember my stomach cramping and my body aching for quite a while.

Even with that experience I still liked spiders. I loved to catch insects like grasshoppers and flies and feed them to the spiders in my backyard or in the woods. I liked letting spiders crawl on me. I liked the tickle of their feet as they crawled around, but after my experience with the black widow I had a pretty good respect for them as well.

In that area of San Diego we had brown recluses, black widows and tarantulas. I actually had a pet tarantula who used to crawl all over me, and I would sometimes let him go free because I knew I could always find him in the woodpile.

All of these creatures are vital to the health and flow of nature and I seemed to know that as a kid, which is why I didn't fear them.

Many of these creatures are called "indicator species" which means when the earth becomes unbalanced these animals die first. It's like sending a canary into a coal mine to see if there are odorless, poisonous gases present. If the bird lives, it's all clear.

When I was a young kid I could go outside every day and have an abundance of small creature encounters. There were countless amphibians, reptiles and bats around. As I grew older and more of their habitat was destroyed for housing, the air and water became more polluted and the amphibians, reptiles and bats all but disappeared.

It seems the most adaptable animals are the ones who can survive in urban areas. Raccoons, opossums, pigeons, doves and coyotes adapt well, but the diversity that is necessary for even these creatures to survive is fast diminishing. There may come a day when even the songbirds will disappear from these areas, but sadly I imagine very few people will notice.

Interestingly, even the plant kingdom has been overtaken. Many species from other countries come into our country on ships, carried as spores or seeds on packaging, and have invaded and killed many of our own indigenous plants. For example, most of the Hawaiian native plants have disappeared due to farming, building and landscaping with non-native plants.

I suppose with a global economy that it's just too difficult to monitor every ship, plane or piece of luggage, and it's too soon to really know how each ecosystem will adjust or not. Yet, I believe if we can take care of our own communities, which include protecting the plant and animal life that exists within it, we are acting responsibly and hopefully bringing our small world into balance.

"No act of kindness, no matter how small, is ever wasted."
-Aesop

"One hundred percent of the shots I don't take…don't go in the goal."

-Wayne Gretsky

ADVENTURE FOR THE SAKE OF THE SOUL

Chapter Ten

Adventure and exploring comes naturally to all beings. Before humans were taken over by technology our small, baby brains yearned for the thrill of rolling over and standing up, walking and running without help. In my childhood, we all played outside and got dirty, dug into creeks like beavers trying to stanch the flow of water. We climbed trees pretending we were pioneers looking toward the horizon of pure adventure. Nature filled us and fed our souls with the nutrients that made us braver, more creative and more inspired. If nature was the food, adventure was the water that kept us hydrated with the possibilities of life's fluidity.

I loved pushing the adventure envelope as a kid. Even today adventure is vital to my well being, though I have learned to temper my adrenaline addictions with the reality of my aging body. Pushing the envelope allows us to connect with our inner strengths and can create a sense of personal power and self-esteem. Adventures help build self-confidence.

In the last twenty years or so that I have been working with kids, I see the effects of well meaning parents who prefer their kids to find safe adventure in computers, and technology and over scheduled, organized sports. The effects are dreadful on a kid's creativity and independence. I believe sports and activities are great for kids, but there needs to be a balance where every minute of the day is not overscheduled. There needs to be room to explore.

Today, the pressure to get into a good school, to create a secure future by their late teens, and out perform their peers is creating a generation of psychologically numb kids.

My observation of today's kids is that they have tighter schedules than their parents, filled with so many after school activities that are supposed to build bodies and imaginations, but in reality it leaves kids stressed, burned out, over programmed and devoid of any creative, individual thought process.

Is it any wonder they turn to drugs – a place where they relax, let their imaginations go and feel no responsibility? But we all know that consistent use of drugs burns them out even more – whole years of crucial, social development are lost in a haze of mind numbing smoke. And yet the initial pleasures found in drugs can be felt drug free in the natural world, and it's a cure that parents ignore.

Tumbling into creeks, getting dirty, exploring woods, crawling up waterfalls, getting muddy, getting lost, getting crazy, climbing a tree are ways kids can express themselves spontaneously and joyfully.

Being open to adventure means being willing to change plans, to change directions, to change your mind, and to learn problem solving skills. I think most people would see that as a tremendous inconvenience and a waste of time. But how much real adventure can a kid get watching television, talking on their cell phones, and playing video games?

Sadly, too many kids when they arrive at Headwaters Outdoor School for the first time are woefully undeveloped. They have been living a virtual life and not really experiencing our world hands on. As they become teenagers, drugs and alcohol become their adventure. It becomes their replacement to that innate call to adventure. Their crazy adventures are not spirit filled, but hurtful and painful to themselves and others.

Time and again I see young adults, who should be flourishing and exploring the world, returning home to live within the "safety" of their parent's homes. I've been seeing an increase in a generation of "lost boys and girls." Fear based parents, who want the best for their children, tend to overprotect them by sheltering them and depriving them of their own life experiences. The results are young adults who struggle later in life to make their own decisions out of fear of making the wrong one. They are paralyzed by false fear. They don't have the experienced, life skills or drive to know that they can get through challenges. The self-confidence just isn't there.

I truly fear a weakening generation. There seems to be a rise in entitlement issues of things a child wants to entertain themselves, and it being handed to them without it being sought after on their own or worked for. In those cases the "reward" never seems to last or is satisfying because they haven't put their own energy into it. To me it would be like being handed a trophy without even competing. It means nothing because their own energy, heart and soul didn't go into it. Everything seems to be about instant gratification.

Parents, let your kids respond to the primal call within their youthful spirits by allowing them adventures in nature. I am still amazed when parents ask me if their child can be killed in nature. We do the most dangerous thing we can do almost every day without thought, we ride in cars. We are more likely to get killed in a car accident on the freeway than we are in nature.

To my shock and deep disappointment I've had school kids come to my land, amongst thousands of amazing trees and be forbidden by their parents to climb them. Even supervised, if I allow those kids to climb the trees the parents will not allow their children to come back to our land. Questions arise about our school's insurance policies. That to me is insanity. A world filled with selfish lawyers and crooked insurance Mongols have dictated our lives.

Life is risk and kids need to learn to meet those challenges head-on. They need to learn how to react quickly in dangerous situations, and they need to learn how to trust their intuition. They are not going to develop these skills sitting dormant indoors.

Once kids are able to get outside more, parents are pleasantly surprised how their child opens up, grows and flourishes when given the opportunities to challenge themselves, and to be free to explore with guidance and a little room.

One of my wonderful death-defying adventures took place after a torrential rainstorm when Stevens Creek, in what is now the Silicon Valley, became a raging river. One of my friends had an old raft collecting dust and spider webs hanging in his garage. It seemed to us the perfect vehicle to ride the raging waters of Stevens Creek. We convinced my father to drive us up to where the creek meets the dam so we could ride it from there into the valley. The peaceful, burbling little creek of summertime was a boiling cauldron of fun.

As I look back, I realize how lucky I was that my dad allowed me to have this kind of adventure. We could have hitchhiked not telling anyone, which in hindsight would not have been very smart. As reluctant as my father was to leave us after seeing the power of the raging creek, he knew it was better to know where we were and let us have such an adventure. I am sure he prayed all the way home as well.

It was a sunny day, so with shirts off and wearing only shorts, we carried the raft down to the creek. The water was about 45 degrees – pretty cold unless you're thirteen. The four of us squeezed on to a 2-person raft. With only two paddles we shoved off from the shore and shot into the creek like a cork out of a champagne bottle. It was dangerous and the cold water kept pouring into the raft while we bailed as fast as we could.

The creek took us through countless private properties, many of which had man-made water hazards of garbage and junk that people had dumped into the creek. At one point as we came around a bend, we saw a length of barbed wire strung about 2 feet above the water. With the protection of the gods for fools and teenagers we ducked within seconds of getting decapitated.

Laughing off that near miss with youthful bravado we came around another bend and hit a big rock that sent us all sailing into the muddy bank. As I crawled up the slippery slope, grabbing at mud like a lifeline, I unearthed a bunch of buried turtle eggs, which was a great discovery that I quickly re-buried.

After the bank dump we rescued our worse-for-wear raft, and with all the excitement of Christmas morning, we piled back on and into the raging waters. With all the dumping and bumping we all began to shiver, laughing at who had the biggest goose bumps. We were too excited to really feel cold. We felt alive and connected to the spirit of a raging river.

Drifting down the creek, we had seen many beautiful pieces of driftwood whizzing past us like loose cannons. We saw dead fish that couldn't survive the rough water. We kept seeing "No Trespassing" signs and thought we would be shot on sight, but I guess we were going too fast for anyone to shoot or care.

When we had finally floated into the flatlands, which at that time were covered with orchards, we gave a victory whoop that could be heard all the way to San Francisco. We recounted as many moments as we could remember. "Remember the barbed wire? How about the frog up there? What about when I got sucked into the rapid and almost drowned - man were your faces white." With all our limbs in tact we took the raft back to the garage to collect dust. We never told my father what happened because he would surely have regretted sending us to our doom if we had drowned. Although, somehow the local paper got wind of our adventure and sent a reporter to do a story on the boys who rafted down Stevens Creek.

Another adventure on San Francisco Bay gave my friend Steve's parents pause about being my friend, as I was always doing daredevil things and this one was too much for them. The bay isn't necessarily a place where you see four boys fishing in a 12-foot dinghy. We had heard the striped bass were running and we wanted to catch some big ones. I had caught a 32-pound bass in the surf off Santa Cruz beach and when the guys saw my fish the spirit of competition was strong, and they wanted their shot at the big fish.

We borrowed a dinghy from a friend's father, made lunches and off we went. We were like the crew in "Gilligan's Island" heading off to an adventure and having no clue where we'd end up. Steve and I knew how to sail so we got into the bay with no trouble, although, with all of us in the boat we were riding a bit low in the water. We weren't catching much the first couple of hours, but the view and playfulness of sea gulls entertained us for quite a while.

Floating peacefully on the water, we told stories, drank our cold drinks and ate our sandwiches. Like most afternoons in the bay the wind picks up pretty good late in the day and our little boat started to pick up speed. The fog rolled in over the hills, looking like squeezed toothpaste from a tube, and it brought the biting wind that made it feel like winter. As the boat increased in speed, it started to take in water and we were getting wet, which with the dense fog started to give us a serious chill, and of course at the most inopportune moment our rudder broke from too much wind and too many people on board. The boat started to spin out of control, but with some presence of mind we got the sail down. Though we were left rudderless and without wind power, we wouldn't capsize.

We had started out at about 10:00 a.m. and it was nearing 8:00 p.m. with the light fading fast. We were definitely not prepared for disaster. We didn't have food or water left or enough life vests, and the only emergency tool was a small flashlight. We tried to signal with it, but the puny light must have been invisible in the waning light. We were beginning to get nervous that we might get hypothermia, as we were still wet and the wind was an unkind partner in this impending disaster, so we huddled together to stay warm. Around 1:30 in the morning someone on another boat finally saw our light and pulled up alongside and called the Coast Guard to rescue us. Steve's parents were really freaked out. My parents were used to my reckless adventures and took it in stride.

We weren't really scared – just really cold. We had a great time and we had great stories for our less adventurous friends. The local paper again got wind of the story and did another article on us. Even today I think that adventure for adventure's sake fills our spirit and inspires us to see and do things we normally don't. Adventure opens doors to greater creativity and allows for grand thoughts and big dreams.

Some of the best adventures that I remember happened when I was a little kid from seven to ten years old. During the Sunnyvale days, when the dark people were around, I would sneak out my window and spend the entire night in the woods while my parent's thought I was peacefully sleeping in my bed. I built shelters to sleep in and felt really safe. I was called to the woods as a way of alleviating the fear of what those people did to me. I listened to the spirit that called me to the safety of the woods and the adventure it provided me.

My favorite stupid, kid adventure happened in Glacier National Park while I was visiting my grandfather. He would often take me to the park and let me wander off to explore on my own. One of those summers when I was about 11 years old, I came across a grizzly sow and her cubs. I had a little Kodak, instamatic camera and I wanted to get a picture of the family. I moved very slowly toward her. She was always aware of my position but kept grazing, keeping her cubs close. As I approached that invisible line of too-close-for-comfort, she turned her body with such a great force that I almost fell backward. Like Gulliver standing up among the Lilliputians, she rose up on her hind legs to an unimaginable height, sniffing and snorting and telling me in no uncertain terms I was not wanted there.

At that age, I had this idea that I could almost walk up and hug bears just because I loved them so much. She was not feeling that love however, and I knew I was in trouble. I didn't know whether I should run to the nearest tree and climb or just stand still. Rather stupidly, I moved closer so I could take a picture, and with that she charged me so fast I didn't have time to react. She stopped about 50 feet from me, but it felt closer, as I could feel her breath on my face. I didn't look her in the eyes, which is probably what saved me. She made a few more grunts, turned and galloped back to her cubs. They all took off so fast across the meadow and disappeared into the trees that it became a blurred dream.

My grandfather was not happy when I told him what had happened; yet, he knew the price of allowing a young boy to venture a field was that there is always danger and risk. He lectured me on the space a bear needs, particularly a mother with her cubs. He did say that to look a bear in the eyes is a sign of confrontation so not looking at her most likely did save my life. On the other hand, I wanted to believe it was my open heart and love for bears that stopped her in her tracks. It was a frightening, but awesome experience for me because I felt that she had somehow come inside me and united with my spirit bear. I was sure it was a sign that bear country was a second home.

The greatest joy I had as a child, and one of the greatest joys I have today is to wander aimlessly in nature. I love to explore and to see what's around the next turn, over the next ledge or deep inside a cave. When I go into nature with an open heart and mind, I am pulled physically and spiritually along as if I have no will of my own. I have had a great life and I believe it is due in great part to giving myself up to the spirit of adventure.

This may not be a confession that as a mentor I should admit, but my personal feeling is that signs are meant to be interpreted. While growing up if I saw a sign that read, no trespassing, to me that meant, great, that means I'm going to be the only one in there. Do we need to use common sense of when situations are too dangerous? Of course we do, but more often than not, there are way too many voices telling us no and not enough asking us, why not?

Adventures always have a degree of risk and I have been willing to risk life's tests in order to live my vision. The risks that I have taken have made me a more creative person and allowed me to have deep relationships with the people I love.

"Keep knocking, and the joy inside will eventually open a window and look out to see who's there."

-*Rumi*

"In the darkest corner of the sky is where the rainbow shines the brightest."

-Julie Boettler

SHELTERS

Chapter Eleven

Shelters of all kinds are amazing testaments to man-kind's creativity. Shelters that are as small as a twig lean-to to the Taj Mahal are structural statements as to who we are. The earth shelters that we build are constructed from what is available in our wilderness environment. They can be some of the most beautiful structures in the world.

My first shelter-building teachers were the woodland animals. I would observe the squirrels, pack rats and beavers busily gathering sticks and piling them on top of each other to create mounds 3 to 4 feet thick. The thickness and height would act as a protective wall from predators. For humans, an earth shelter creates security, protection from the elements and a wonderful home. It gives us a sense of comfort.

I would make small debris huts by putting up a ridge pole and stacking branches on top of that. To insure a weatherproof structure, I would cover the branches with debris like pine needles, dried ferns, moss or bark. A fancier structure called a wickiup, consisted of small trees and saplings covered with outer layers of bark. Some of my shelters even had more than one room.

My favorite shelters when I was a kid were dug into the earth. They could only be reached by crawling under the roots and into an underground space, which was cool in the summer and relatively warm in the winter. I had shelters along creeks and shelters on hillsides overlooking valleys. Over time I had a network of shelters scattered over a wide ranging territory that were rarely seen by other people, but were havens for me when I explored.

The important thing about a shelter is that it allows a person to feel at home in the wilderness. They gave me places of my own where I could center myself and find peace. I always kept my shelters clean and made them beautiful and fitting with the environment. A good shelter can blend with the environment and look like an earth sculpture.

I built one of my favorite shelters in my own back yard. When the developers started to cut down the forests and fruit orchards in the Silicon Valley, I decided to befriend them in order to scrounge their left over scraps. I would get plywood, two-by-fours, nails, old windows and even roofing material. A couple of friends and I would haul the "booty" to my back yard where we built a three story structure next to the pond that I had made.

This make-shift hotel had sleeping quarters, a living room and a room at the very top that had a sensational view and a deck. It had a locked door and you had to crawl up the middle on a pole to get to any of the levels. I decorated the outside with bird feeders, and put a telescope on the top deck so we could watch the stars on clear nights. I papered the walls with nature pictures that I'd torn from well read National Geographic magazines. One of my rooms was papered with old maps from that magazine as well. A third room had all kinds of art objects that I'd found in nature. I collected unique pieces of wood, flowers and leaves that became dried arrangements, and animal bones and skins with skulls and teeth that looked like sculptures.

I often made my shelters so a fire could be built within them. I would also build them near creeks as often as possible so that I could have fresh water. Playing around like that really taught me about the basic necessities of life, and it taught me how to be creative with what was available. It inspired me to think bigger and deepened my connection with nature.

I believe that shelter building is the best way to engage city people in being comfortable in the woods. Most people are incredibly creative if you leave them alone in the woods to create their own shelter. Many adults at my school become kids again when they build their shelters. It reminds them of their fort building days as a kid, and while they are creating their space it seems they have an endless internal and external smile.

I encourage them to always treat their shelter as a sacred space. I also encourage them when they go backpacking to build natural shelters to sleep in, without damaging their surroundings, and take them down and leave no trace when they leave. I tell them if they want to bring a tent as back up when they first go out that's ok, but to also challenge themselves in different environments with a variety of natural materials. And if they get cold or wet then they will have learned a lesson for the next time.

Shelter building is one of my favorite creative times to play. And yes, I have spent many nights in the cold and soaking rain as I was growing up, learning what not to do, but what great stories to tell.

When I was older, my Uncle Bill would take me up to the deep snow in the mountains of Colorado to teach me how to build shelters in an inhospitable environment. I started out digging holes in the snow, which eventually became snow caves. We made snow caves that had two or three rooms connecting them by a network of tunnels.

The movie that inspired me most during that time was *Nanook of the North*. Nanook was an Inuit who lived in Alaska and built this incredible igloo from blocks that he had carved from the ice. The best touch however was the window he made from a sheet of clear ice. My uncle and I actually took inspiration from that movie and we built an igloo from snow and cut the blocks just like Nanook. We built our igloo into a spiral shape, leaving two holes for windows that we made by cutting chunks of ice from the frozen lake.

There is no reason for people who are stranded for a time in the wilderness to ever die from exposure. Lost children for example naturally go with their instincts. When tracking lost children more often than not they are perfectly fine, balled up under brush with debris keeping them warm enough to survive. There have been adult hunters however, who when lost, panicked and wandered too far and got hypothermia. In their frozen state of delusion they were found dead, sitting exposed in the open extremes.

The simplest thing in the world is to use the materials available to build a home that keeps you dry and relatively safe. Observe the animals around you. Where are they building their shelters and what are they building them with? Take advantage of fallen logs and hollowed out trees. Watch to avoid low ditches that may fill up with rain water. Become a part of the environment you're in and blend in.

I highly recommend going into your local woods or park and start building. Camouflage your shelter and see how many people even know you're there. You'll get an insight as to how aware, or not, we humans are. I will also give you a little hint. Most humans never look up. You may have to get a little creative and build a temporary structure due to local laws, but don't let that stop you from having fun.

"For those who believe, no proof is necessary. For those who don't believe, no proof is possible."

- John St. Clair Thomas

SPIRITUALITY THROUGH NATURE

Chapter Twelve

When I was about 10 years old I had my first experience with a "calling" while visiting my grandfather in Montana. I didn't really understand what the urge was inside me, but I knew that I was supposed to do something. Whatever it was, it was a good feeling. I had been going through the horrors with the dark people for a couple of years and I had become accustomed to fear and bad feelings, so a feeling that was good when I was not immersed in nature was not really normal.

While I was cleaning the chicken coop one day, that good urge kept at me like an insistent fly. When I finished with my chores I decided to just wander and to let the urge or the feeling take me wherever it would. I wandered along the rough, dirt track that disappeared into the thick cedar and pine woods. About a mile from my grandfather's farm I found a clearing at the end of the footpath. In the clearing was a rounded structure with a big fire pit in front of it. Flathead Indians from the neighboring ranches were there hanging out, talking and stoking the fire. I was fascinated. It seemed like a scene from one of my books about the old west and I had stepped back in time.

I watched from what I thought was a hidden spot, but one of the Indians had seen me. He had beautiful, black hair that hung in a braid down his back, and wore a beat up "ol' timer's" hat, which was pulled down tight and covered his ears. His eyes were a deep brown and gentle, and seemed to twinkle with a welcome, pulling me from my hiding place and into their world.

All the Indians were friendly and each one told me a bit about what they were doing. They told me it was a sweat lodge made from bent willow and alder sticks and covered with canvas. It was a dome shape with an entry low to the ground because they humbled themselves to "mother earth" when they entered into her earthly womb. The rocks were heated in the pit until they were red-hot. They were the medium that acted in concert with the water when it was poured over them to create the steam. The steam bathed their bodies cleaning their skin and creating enough heat that their bodies would sweat out any poisons, both physical and emotional. The door was closed while this happened so they could pray and sing in darkness as if they had gone back into the body that gave them life. When they emerged, they would be re-born, regenerated and reinvigorated to deal with life's daily troubles.

My family was Catholic, and the rigors of Sunday Catholicism wore heavy on me as a kid. I was hard pressed to dress up for the heavenly fathers, and I figured if that's what Jesus and God wanted then I was one of the flock's black sheep, as I preferred the earth's dirt to altar boy robes. I remember thinking that there must be something more to religion than a priest telling us all how sinful we were. It never seemed to fit for me. My youthful experiences in nature suggested that there wasn't anything bad or evil in nature. Everything seemed to have its place and its purpose, and there wasn't any one "thing" telling any other "thing" what to do. They all seemed to just be and interact.

The Indians told me that the sweat lodge was one of their religious practices and they invited me to join. The difference between their practice and my family's was certainly not lost on my young psyche. I knew when I entered the lodge and the door flap was lowered that I had crawled into something big that would effect me the rest of my life. I sat in silence, listening to the chants and prayers in a language that I didn't speak or understand, yet the sounds and the music helped me transcend from not knowing to knowing.

I spent many summers sweating with the Flatheads. I was always quiet and overwhelmed because I was the only white person and a kid; yet, they were always welcoming and eager to teach me about the spirituality that exists in every living thing.

My new mentors taught me that Mother Earth's heartbeat is replicated by the drumbeat. They taught me that things found in nature such as rocks, feathers, bones, sticks, etc. could and did have spiritual power and energy. They placed their sacred items on an altar that was created from rock and wood and placed prominently in front of the lodge between the lodge and the fire. They called these items medicine items and placed them in bags or pouches called bundles. They carried them until the power of the object was no longer needed, and then they gave them back to the earth or gave them away to others who might need the power and the energy. They taught me that these items are not really ours to own and the more we hoard their power, the quicker that power dissipates. They believed in giving away the things they deeply cared about.

That special group of men deeply impressed upon my mind the power and spirit that pervade a clean, organized and beautiful camp or ceremonial area. They taught me that function and beauty were inseparable.

Drums, fire-making kits, shelters, rattles and pipes worked better when time was spent on making them beautiful, thereby bringing in both spirit and life. I learned how to be creative by making things from nature. I learned to communicate with the object by shutting down my chatty brain and allowing my intuition to guide my hand as I carved a piece of wood or rock.

Ultimately, what I took on as my spiritual practice was taught to me by those men who collectively became my spiritual teachers. What I chose to believe in wasn't just because they said so, but it was because it felt right for me. It resonated with me, and the practices I learned and use today are tools to help me with my own direct connection with what I call spirit.

I was able to take their teachings home and share them with my friends who thought it was really cool to do "Indian" stuff. We built a small sweat lodge in my backyard by collecting willow branches and making a dome shaped frame, which we covered with sheets, blankets and a canvas tarp. We picked herbs from my mother's garden, sage from the Santa Cruz Mountains and bay leaves from the trees in the redwood forest. When dried we would put them on the hot rocks in the sweat where the smoke would cover us like a sacred blanket.

The Flatheads taught me that screaming and yelling and having fun was just as sacred as praying and singing. My friends and I did plenty of both, and for over 40 years I have used the sweat lodge personally, and in the school to help students understand the connection between ceremony and spirituality.

I had assumed that since I had a calling at such an early age that everyone did. As I got older and shared my hopes and dreams with my friends, I was surprised that they hadn't had such an experience. In my teens, most of my friends just assumed they would follow in their father's footsteps or just go to college and see what happened. They never seemed to have hunches about what they would do with their lives or they didn't recognize a moment of intuition.

We were never taught to respect our intuitive feelings. As a matter of fact, I remember quite the opposite when I was a kid. I remember adults telling me that a hunch is not a fact and the world is based on fact. Gratefully, that all seemed to change in the late 1950's, and certainly the 1960's was all about dropping out and getting in touch with our inner selves. Transcendental meditation became one of the tools of the 60's generation.

I think I was able to key into inner knowingness and intuition very early because of the physical and mental torture I experienced and witnessed at the hands of our neighbors. I became hyper-aware of my environment and subsequently very aware of my feelings. I found my release and my peace in nature where I felt more at "one" with everything wild, than with people. I felt that God had talked to me through the spirit of plants and animals and I felt the mystery. I have always trusted my inner knowing and my intuitions, and I have always been rewarded with rich experiences.

The physical beauty of the high sierra has always struck me. In middle school I hadn't hiked above tree level very much. When I had finally talked my dad into taking me to my teacher, Mr. Robertson's, special fishing spot, I could feel a tingling on the back of my neck. I knew when I got there how sacred a space it was. It was an amazing amphitheater. The few trees that were there grew out of the cracks and were low and gnarly looking, finding survival and life in the harshest of environments.

Because the climb to this special place was not often taken by people back then the wildlife was abundant. I imagined that Lewis and Clark and the other great adventurers who traveled the great expanse of America before it was settled, had the same visions of wildlife, though their visions were far more populated with all kinds of animals. As I climbed I pretended that I was the first person discovering this part of America. I was the first human to see these white, granite peaks where the marmots, deer and mountain lions prowled for food.

The ragged edges of stone melted into green meadows and wet lands, filled with the deafening croak of the frogs. Snakes slithered along the banks easily catching their singing prey, while golden eagles, hawks and falcons flew above waiting for just the right moment to dive for their dinner. I had died, and each step was taking me closer to heaven. The grandeur of the little creeks filtering out of the glaciers, and the banks of melting snow with wildflower sprouts popping through the snow filled me with such happiness, that I would sometimes roll around in the grass screaming with joy. I couldn't remember ever having such a strong connection to the earth than at that moment, and I knew that I had had some really strong connections. But this, this was ecstasy, and I was drunk on the earth's vibrating energy and color.

My father and my friend thought that I had gone mad, and for a brief few hours I had. I had been called to a spot that had transported me to another realm of existence, and it still transports me when I go there to this day. It is the number one spirit place for me and I rue the day when I am too old to make the climb.

This is the place where I also really learned how to gather food or sustenance for the soul. We know how to harvest food from the earth. Some of us know how to identify wild edible plants that would feed us if no backpack food were available, or as a way to augment our backpack supply; yet, how many of us know how to feed the soul?

We all appreciate a beautiful sunset or a full moon. Most people like to stroll along manicured paths that take us through gardens or woods, and some of us even like to get off the path. These are all things that connect us momentarily to nature and to the mystery of a world, of a universe that is larger than just us. But feeding the soul is about gathering the spirit and essence, the "medicine" of a place and of things. It's about sitting and looking at nothing and everything. It's about wandering with no destination in mind. Sometimes as you wander you feel so absolutely connected to that place that you wonder if you might have dreamed it into existence.

I have experienced incredible rainbows. I have walked paths in the wilderness with wild animals that chose to be in close proximity to me, rather than run away or hide. I have felt the cry of birds that echoed deep inside me. These moments are sacred moments in nature. They are the earth's life force letting us know that we too belong. All of those experiences are a part of who I am now. They have come into me and as a result I share that energy with everyone I connect with. We all do that. We are the sum of all those rainbows, sunrises, sunsets and sacred moments that we stop and take in.

How many sacred moments have you experienced when you're frantic or rushing or gabbing away with friends? They happen when we are silent or alone. Like an incredible gourmet meal, all the senses are involved. The eyes see the beauty, the nose smells the aromas and the tongue tastes the flavors.

One such spiritual, gourmet moment happened for me when I had taken a needed break from hiking to my sacred spot. I watched a bolt of lightning explode on the mountaintop. The impact sent a rock falling down the cliff, which hit another rock and another until the power of the rocks created a landslide. It flooded the side of the mountain with the flow of rock on rock and then just as quickly as it began it stopped. I sat awestruck and grateful that I had taken that moment to sit.

Another powerful way to experience your self in nature is to do a vision quest. Indians in all cultures use it at different times in their lives to find their next step. As I mentioned, my first vision quest was on Mt. Shasta when I was 13 years old, and it was then that I wrote my code of honor. I have had many vision quests since that first one in many different places.

A quest must be a spot in nature that is removed from your normal environment. It can be in the desert or on a mountain, by a lake or in the woods. It is a place where few if any people go. It's a place that you choose, where you can sit for 2-4 days in quiet with no food and no distractions of the man-made kind. It's a time to attune your self to the rhythm of nature, which is slow to slower. It's a time to listen to the chatter in your brain, which keeps you busy and moving fast, but when paid close attention to is just babble. It's a time to clear out all the garbage so you can heed the deeper inner messages and intuitions that you would normally not even know were there.

On one of my quests at Robertson Lake, I was sitting in a crevice up a hillside along a little creek praying and asking the Great Spirit and the nature spirits to help me. After two days of praying and asking, I had pretty much depleted my prayers. I decided with the last couple of days left I would just observe. I watched the sun's progress move ever so slowly across the sky. I watched and listened to the birds and insects. Everything moved so slowly that my mind and my thoughts became equally as slow, and from this slowness emerged the thought that I should be teaching people about nature. I had always informed or taught, but it wasn't until I created Headwaters Outdoor School in 1992 that I realized the power of that quiet moment.

The beauty of the soul feasting on nature is that there is no right or wrong and you can't over eat. Nature is the great teacher with no agenda, no dogma and plenty of room for everyone. Nature teaches us that when we humans remove ourselves from the web of life, we lose control. We get crazy and anxious. Right now, Mother Earth is trying to teach us that as her body heats up, our food source, both physical and spiritual, will become extinct. Some of us are listening and taking action, but sadly not enough yet to make her better.

"A human being is part of the whole, called by us Universe, a part limited in time and space. He experiences himself, his thoughts and feelings as something separated from the rest-a kind of optical delusion of his consciousness. This delusion is a kind of prison for us, restricting us to our personal desires and to affection for a few persons nearest to us. Our task must be to free ourselves from this prison by widening our circle of compassion to embrace all living creatures and the whole of nature in its beauty."

-Albert Einstein

"The breeze at dawn has secrets to tell you-don't go back to sleep. You must ask for what you really want-don't go back to sleep. People are going back and forth across the doorsill where the two worlds touch, the door is round and open-don't go back to sleep."

-Rumi

INTO THE WILDERNESS

Chapter Thirteen

It was an unusually dark, overcast day. It seemed as if night was fast approaching at mid-day. My backpack was heavy as I was just starting my journey, and I wondered if I should make camp early or keep moving. As I walked through unfamiliar terrain I wondered if any human had walked where I was walking. I must have been a hundred miles or more from any road – paved or dirt. As I secured my .22 rifle, that I used to shoot small game, and my fishing rod on the side of my backpack, I decided that even with the approaching storm it would be better to hike to a good camping site rather than huddle under rocks on the ridge where I had been traveling.

As I came down the ridgeline, I stopped cold, as I had come upon what were decidedly fresh, wolf tracks. I was both exhilarated and afraid at the same time. I had dreamed of the wolves coming and laying down with me at night. I had imagined that they would know that I would never hurt them, and they would befriend me and protect me on my wilderness journey. Of course, daydreams and reality collide with the sight of fresh tracks. I stood very still and listened for branches breaking or any other audible sign that they could be close. I scanned the sky for ravens to see if perhaps a fresh kill was close by. As much as I loved wolves I didn't want to happen upon a pack of hungry wolves around a fresh kill.

I was 17 years old when I had decided that I would go to the Canadian wilderness to live off the land. I had seen a National Geographic film on the Nahanni River in the Northwest Territories explored by river rafters, and I knew that's where I wanted to go. My years spent with many mentors had prepared me for what I was to create. It was going to be my true Rite of Passage from high school into the world. It would be a four-month walkabout, a spiritual journey that would take me into the deepest parts of nature, within the wilderness, and within myself.

It's funny how the power of some experiences in life don't reveal themselves immediately – how years can pass or even decades pass before the power of such a moment in time can be felt. As I write this book about my life and my life in nature, I realize how truly profound it was at that age to plan such a solo journey, and I am only now aware of how it was the defining moment in my life.

I had graduated from high school early, not because I was a genius, but because I hated school. I was uninspired and unsupported for who I was. Realizing that and being a doer and a problem solver, I took as many extra classes as I could. I studied hard and did a good job, and escaped the confines of those stifling walls in April, which is when I headed north to Canada.

I had an old Datsun pick-up outfitted with a camper shell, loaded with gear and food. I was a traveling universe unto myself. I headed up the North Coast Trail where I spent a couple of weeks hiking through wilderness beauty of the coastal rainforest. I traveled through Glacier National Park on to Jasper and Banff, and then north of Banff where true wilderness begins and the towns get further and further apart.

After driving a couple of days on dirt roads past the last of the old mining towns, I reached a spot where I could hike into the Nahanni River. Though only about two miles separated me from the last town and the wilderness, it was a two mile eternity. I found the perfect off-road spot to park the truck, where I camo'd the hell out of it with willow branches and long grass. I did have the presence of mind to leave a note on the dashboard telling where I was going, and to not tow it away.

I decided to stay in that area for a few days and scout for animal tracks to get a sense of what was around and what I should be looking out for. I was fortunate that the tracks next to the river were plentiful, and told a story of the daily lives of all the four legged creatures in the area. I was delighted to find wolverine tracks, as I respected the wolverines for their aggressiveness and their elusiveness. They embody pure wilderness – so rarely seen in nature – they are efficient hunters and fearless, even facing down predators larger than themselves. It was a goal of mine to actually see a wolverine, and over the four months I saw numerous tracks, but only glimpsed one from high on a ridge as it traveled a valley below.

I can hardly put into words the exhilaration I felt just being in that camp. It had been my life's dream to be in country where I was the intruder, where bear, wolf and wolverine were the prominent inhabitants. It was equally exhilarating as there were no other people in the campsite. I was the last man standing, the last man on earth, and rather than fear I felt a complete state of grace. I was home.

I studied the topo maps religiously, as there were no known trails. I had to depend upon my innate sense of direction, but I also believed for me there was no such thing as being lost in the wilderness. I was wandering and adventuring and experiencing. I also had the river as my guide and benchmark, and the mountain peaks were as good as road signs. I observed the direction of the sun as it traversed the sky.

Light is a wonderful tool – its fusion with the earth and plants is different everywhere we go. As an amateur photographer at that point, I was captivated by light. The sun's play through the trees in the morning, afternoon and evening was subtle, but observably different there versus other campsites I chose.

One of my major concerns on the trip became one of my greatest joys. I loved fishing – I mean I loved fishing. I lived for fishing. I knew that in order to get the protein I needed I would have to find fish. I had experienced from California rivers and lakes that abundant fish could be a hit or miss thing. Not so here. I not only didn't have any problems, but it seemed whenever I dipped my line into the river pools a fish would be caught before the lure hit the water. I could catch fish with my bare hands, not quite so easily as with my line, but if I was patient and hid in the shade by the river's edge I could observe and grab. It tested my quickness of eye and muscles, and was just plain fun. With that concern so quickly dispelled it left me more time to spend observing the animals and plants and exploring.

It had been my intent from the beginning to track grizzly bears. I had been inspired by the famous naturalist Craighead family who did just that - tracked and recorded grizzly bear activity in Wyoming and Montana. I knew that the bears in this area were seldom hunted so they didn't have the same kind of fear of humans that black bears or even grizzlies have/had in the U.S. But I also knew enough about the great grizzlies to keep my distance and to let my presence be known quietly and calmly.

If we can be reincarnated from animals, I am the reincarnation of a bear. I look like a bear, I eat like a bear, I play like a bear, I am quick to anger like a bear, I even smell like a bear at times and I certainly snore like a bear. Tracking bear in Canada was like going home to reunite with my brothers.

I was fortunate to find the tracks of a female grizzly and her cubs. I followed them for a good two weeks. Most likely because it was summer and food was plentiful in the verdant and densely vegetative valleys, their range was more compact than the 100 square miles I had heard bears need, so when I lost their tracks, I knew to scout the riverbeds until I picked them up again. I knew they liked to fish and I knew they needed the water, so the mud prints were stepping stones to the living treasure.

One particular afternoon, I had been following her and the cubs at a safe distance through a breathtaking meadow full of late, spring wildflowers and rich, lush grasses. She and the cubs were cruising the riverbed below. One of the cubs was splashing in the river honing his or her fishing skills, and the other cub was a distance from them, closer to me. I inched my way down the hillside. I knew that the mother was aware of my presence, as she would occasionally stand on her back legs, a towering figure of fur and muscle, and huff and snort in my direction. I got within about 100 feet of her, hiding behind a big rock in the middle of the meadow, but she knew where I was and she was getting very nervous. She started chomping her teeth, and huffing and grunting for her cubs to come near. I suppose she could smell me as well, and when the cubs didn't respond to her, her grunting and huffing became more intense and angry. I figured at that point I should show myself, hoping that it would calm her down a bit. I stood up and walked about a foot away from the rock so she could clearly see and smell me. I knew enough to not look at her, so my eyes were downcast, and between the blink of an eye and the next she was two feet from me.

Her breath was hot and putrid, and I literally had to freeze every muscle so that I wouldn't run. I thought I hadn't had time for fear until I felt the warm rush of urine down the side of my leg. But through it all, I was certain she wouldn't kill me. We were kindred spirits. I hoped she felt it too.

As quickly as she had charged me, she turned and barked at her cubs to follow her across the river and up the hill. It was so quick and scary and exhilarating, and one of the most memorable moments of my life. It was a peak experience, which for me means that the great mystery, that is nature, creates a small opening that allows you to feel the connection with all things. In that moment, all things are connected in a state of grace - it's perhaps the place where we touch God, and where we understand that we are not only a small part of something so much bigger, but as small as we are we are also necessary.

Many years have passed, but the memories of that time are as fresh and pronounced as the tracks in the river bank mud. I wonder who I would have become if I hadn't had that adventure at that time in my life. As I reflect on why and how I have been able to live so many of my dreams, I realize that I followed my inspirations, rather than the usual drumbeat of societal dictates to go to college, get a nine to five job, earn money, raise a family, retire and wonder way too late where it all went.

I also wonder why as a society we try to redirect a young person's inspirations. We certainly recognize inspiration in gifted children because they are so much further ahead than their peers – be it in math and science or the arts – but we ignore the less pronounced inspirations of the so called normal child. The gift my parents gave me, whether wittingly or not, was the freedom to pursue what inspired me, rather than their expectation of what they thought should have inspired me.

While sitting around a camp fire at night and seeing the illuminated eyes of the wolves from the light of the fire, survival was more prevalent in my mind than inspiration. The howl of the wolves at night is both chilling and beautiful. The beauty of primal communication resonated at the base of my spine. It traveled like hot liquid into my gut, surging toward my throat and finally hitting the electrical impulses of reason in my brain, where fear automatically took over. I wanted to howl a response, but I was afraid I would make them mad by my arrogance.

After about a week of faceless, glowing eyes by the fire, I came to the realization that these "characters" had no intention of eating me. They were just curious. Wolves by mythic connotation have a bad rap. In reality they have loving family units that take excellent, loving care of their young. They are simple creatures that need the companionship of the pack to thrive.

I realized that a good howl might be good for all of us, so I bellowed in a bad wolf accent. I was a little disappointed that the wolves didn't respond, but I think it was because they were laughing too hard. Yet, from that moment on I lost my fear, and though I never really saw them up close, I could feel their presence most of the time I was in the woods. I felt they protected and looked after me, and for no other reason than I was a source of amusement for them, and a kindred spirit.

After some initial loneliness, I acclimated to the silence, or rather the lack of city noise. There was plenty of noise in the woods, but it had a rhythm and cadence that was meditative and calming. There was the occasional screech and blood-curdling cry of an animal meeting its predatory maker. Those jarring sounds kept me aware and vigilant, but not fearful, and they blended with the mellow sound of life as usual.

Over the course of the next couple of months, I encountered many grizzlies, mostly from a distance, wolverine, countless birds, foxes, ubiquitous squirrels and chipmunks. I fished to the point where I became the fish, and knew its hiding spots and habits.

As fall approached I knew my time in that sacred place was coming to an end. I felt a deep sorrow at having to leave the forest, and all the creatures that had become my friends. I felt totally accepted by all the animals, and the plants, and the trees, and even the insects.

Nature's pace is slow but the time passed way too quickly. I was certain that this was how mankind was meant to live – in concert and harmony with nature. I knew that I would never be afraid to be in nature for long periods of time, but I also knew that living as I did so close to the heart and spirit of the earth for all those months would never happen again. It was an initiation into the next path that I would take.

Though by nature I prefer more of a solitary lifestyle, life had different plans for me that I needed to listen to. That period was the beginning inspiration and training for Headwaters Outdoor School. Though it took some years, I knew I wanted to teach people that nature was a place of reverence, a place that accepts our deepest sorrows and transforms them into inspiration if we open our hearts, and rid our minds of silly preconceived ideas. As soon as I opened up to that calling fully the special land where I live now, at the foot of the same mountain where I culminated my rite of passage, came to me through a series of unplanned events.

There are no accidents, and miracles do happen. The mountain called me home, and I've been returning the favor by bringing people back home to nature here ever since. My life has come full circle from a child climbing a mountain, consciously being initiated into an adult, to an adult living at the base of that same mountain over forty years later, initiated into a man of service, living my beliefs and my vision.

My father gave me the gift of trust in allowing me to climb Mt. Shasta to help build the man I am today. He looked after me in the way he knew how that was best for me. In return, after my mother died, I moved my father to my home and had the pleasure of watching over him for the last seven years of his life in this beautiful place on our beloved land, in the shadow of that sacred peak. There is a certain comfort in knowing life and this incredible earth take care of you, and it all comes back around.

People ask me how I have been able to have so many peak experiences out in nature throughout my life, and continue to, and the only answer is that I'm out there. I'm out in those magic hours, out before the sun rises to watch the colors wake up the landscape and hear the gathering of the birds. I'm out at sunset while most people are eating dinner in front of the T.V. and I'm watching the animals emerge from the shadowed edges of the meadow. I get off the trail, and climb trees, and stop to see what is under the next log. In those moments when others think nothing is happening, I wait. I sit and wait and the show begins. It never fails.

On a photography shoot I stop and put the camera down to listen to a pack of wolves echo through the fog misted trees, and watch a herd of elk trample the dewy meadow, escaping the haunting calls, and while standing there caught up in the wonder of life, I find myself surrounded by a herd of bison, being absorbed up within their community as one of them. There is no magic or special quality in me. I just show up, and stay open with curiosity, and it all comes to me, and I become the land and the land becomes me, as it could for anyone. There are no short cuts. Get out in the woods! It's the best place to be.

So where do we go from here? How do we make a difference now? We need to stop abusing, controlling and manipulating the one mother who serves us all so well. Go into the wild, listen, listen, listen and then follow what you *feel*. Everything we need and will ever need has been provided abundantly by nature. Nature is food for the soul, and I have much gratitude for growing up with a soul full of nature.

About The Author

Tim Corcoran's Irish heritage, as taught to him by his uncle and grandfather, has linked him deeply to Earth people's philosophy of life. He first went to woods at age six. He knew then that it was his home. At seventeen he spent four months alone in the Canadian Wilderness practicing Earth living skills.

Tim began a career teaching wildlife conservation in 1974. During this time he learned how to communicate with the spirits of the animals he worked with, enhancing his abilities to connect on an intimate level with them.

He has an extensive background in working with wildlife. He has worked at the Alberta Game Farm in Alberta, Canada as an animal caretaker, the Crandon Park Zoo in Miami Florida as an animal relocation director, and Marine World Africa U.S.A. as a chimp and elephant trainer. Tim co-founded the Native Animal Rescue in Santa Cruz, California, rescuing and releasing injured wildlife. He also took that opportunity to speak at schools to educate hundreds of children on wildlife conservation.

In the late 1980's Tim started a wilderness school in Santa Cruz called Pathfinders, where he led wilderness survival backpack trips and vision quests. As that school grew, in 1992 Tim created Headwaters Outdoor School in Mount Shasta, California to realize his lifelong vision of sharing what he has learned from nature, and to inspire people to discover their own connection with the Earth. Tim teaches outdoor living skills to kids and adults.

Throughout Tim's many years of travels he has become an accomplished professional photographer, and in 2006 he opened the Tim Corcoran Photography Gallery in Mount Shasta, California. His first nature photography book of the Mt. Shasta area will be published in 2011.

Tim lives with his wife, Jean and their pack of dogs on an amazing piece of wooded land in Mount Shasta, California where he runs his outdoor school.

To reach Tim directly please log onto the Headwaters website:

www.hwos.com

For more information on Tim's nature photography please log onto his gallery website: www.timcorcoranphoto.com

"One final paragraph of advice: Do not burn yourselves out. Be as I am- a reluctant enthusiast…a part time crusader, a half-hearted fanatic. Save the other half of yourselves and your lives for pleasure and adventure. It is not enough to fight for the land, it is even more important to enjoy it. While you can. While it's still here. So get out there and hunt and fish and mess around with your friends, ramble out yonder and explore the forests, encounter the grizz, climb the mountains, bag the peaks, run the rivers, breathe deep of that yet sweet and lucid air, sit quietly for a while and contemplate the precious stillness, that lovely, mysterious and awesome space. Enjoy yourselves, keep your brain in your head and your head firmly attached to the body, the body active and alive, and I promise you this much: I promise you this one sweet victory over our enemies, over those deskbound people with their hearts in a safe deposit box and their eyes hypnotized by desk calculators. I promise you this: you will outlive the bastards."

Edward Abbey

LaVergne, TN USA
22 March 2011
221230LV00001B/13/P